Sue Lawrence won Masterchef in 1991 and was the President of the Guild of Food Writers from 2004 to 2007. She wrote a regular column for *Scotland on Sunday* and *Scotland* magazine and was also the *Sunday Times* food columnist. She has written for *Sainsbury's Magazine*, *Woman & Home*, *Country Living* and *BBC Good Food* magazine and appears regularly on radio and television talking about Scottish food and traditions. She won the Regional Writer Glenfiddich Food and Drink Award in 2003 for her work in *Scotland on Sunday*. She is the author of *Sue Lawrence's Book of Baking*, *Scottish Kitchen*, *A Cook's Tour of Scotland* and the award-winning *Scots Cooking*.

Sue lives in Edinburgh with her husband and three children.

Praise for Sue and her previous books:
'Edinburgh's own domestic goddess – the best home-cook in the land' Elisabeth Luard, *Scotsman*

'One of my favourite cookery writers' Darina Allen

'Imaginative cooking of impeccable taste and intelligence. An exceptional book' Richard Ehrlich, *Guardian* [on *Scottish Kitchen*]

'Sue Lawrence's recipes always work. She is a particularly fine baker' Clarissa Dickson Wright

'One of the country's finest food writers' Orlando Murrin, *Daily Express*

'She is one heck of a baker – do try her muffins, cakes and shortbreads' *Sainsbury's Magazine*

'Full of inspiring recipes' *Olive* [on *Book of Baking*]

'The recipes work and the results are delicious' *Sainsbury's Magazine*

'One of the best recipe-writers in the land' Jill Dupleix, *The Times*

TASTE YE BACK

GREAT SCOTS
AND THE FOOD THAT MADE THEM

SUE LAWRENCE

hachette
SCOTLAND

For Isabelle, dear friend since 1963, with love

First published in 2009 by HACHETTE SCOTLAND, an imprint of Hachette UK

1

Contributors' photography ©: eatscotland.com (p2); Lorenzo Agius (p8); Brian Aris (pp42 & 100); Andy Siddens (p56); James Wilson/Evelyn Glennie (p90); Wilhelm Reinke (p96); Julian Broad (p128); David Peat (p130); Denise Else (p140); Paul King (p176)

Cataloguing in Publication Data is available from the British Library ISBN: 978 0 7553 1863 6

Edited by Helena Caldon
Food styling by Maxine Clark
Food photography by Alan Donaldson
Designed and typeset by Republic Productions
Printed by Mohn Media Books, Germany

Hachette Scotland's policy is to use papers that are natural, renewable and recyclable products and made from wood grown in sustainable forests. The logging and manufacturing processes are expected to conform to the environmental regulations of the country of origin.

HACHETTE SCOTLAND
An Hachette UK Company, 338 Euston Road, London NW1 3BH
www.hachettescotland.co.uk www.hachette.co.uk

Acknowledgements

Special thanks to Sir Sean Connery, for not only telephoning me to wish me well for this book, but also for making my daughter Jessica's day as she was home alone, so able to chat to this Great Scot.

Thanks to:

Anna and Bob Anderson	Andy Hall	Judi and John Matheson
Scott Begbie	Dorothy Hilsley	Rob Mitchell
Colin Campbell	Margot Hudson	Angela Morton
Jan Gaffney	Kenneth Hume	Flora and Alan Sharp
John Gordon	John Inverdale	Rory Steel
Vivienne Grant	Isabel Johnson	Rosalind Woolfson
Elisabeth, Jackie and Sue Hadden	Bea Macdonald	

And for lending props:

Joyce Clark; Norman Lee; Timothy Hardie at Rait Village Antique Centre for letting us have the antique plaids; Bob Templeman, Scottish Antiques and Arts Centre, Abernyte and Doune; and Catherine Brown for lending one of her many girdles – a peat fire girdle for the Tattie Scones.

And also a special mention to:

Jenny Brown, literary agent extraordinaire; Bob McDevitt for his publishing vision; Maxine Clark for her brilliant food styling; Alan Donaldson for his wonderful photos; Wendy McCance and Helena Caldon for their proficient editing; and all the team at CHAS, in particular to Kerry and Roslyn. The Children's Hospice Association Scotland (CHAS) is a Scottish charity established to provide hospice services in Scotland for children and young people with life-limiting conditions. A children's hospice offers professional care, practical help and emotional support to the whole family usually from the day of acceptance, to the death of their child, and beyond. For further information, please see www.chas.org.uk

Finally, to Pat, Euan, Faith and Jessica Lawrence. Thanks, as ever, for putting up with the many Highs and occasional Lows of the resident author.

Foreword
by Ewan McGregor

When Sue Lawrence first approached me to ask if I would like to be included in her book, I was absolutely delighted. Not only did it allow me the opportunity to reminisce about the delicious home-cooked food I enjoyed as a child growing up in Crieff, but it also gave me the opportunity to show my support for the Children's Hospice Association Scotland (CHAS), a wonderful Scottish charity which has a very special place in my heart.

I have so loved reading, as I'm sure will you, the tales of the food enjoyed by Scotland's 'great and good' which Sue has researched and recorded in this book.

I would like to thank everyone who contributed and gave their time to talk to Sue and share their fond, or not so fond, memories with her. Finally I'd like to thank Sue for coming up with such a wonderful idea and for her kindness with this great book in choosing to support CHAS.*

Children's Hospice Association Scotland
Sharing the Caring

* At Sue's request, the publisher, Headline Publishing Group Limited ('HPG') has donated £1000 from her advance and will donate 1% of the total royalty income to Children's Hospice Association Scotland (registered charity number: SC019724 – 'CHAS'). HPG will not be paid by CHAS in respect of these donations.

What is patriotism but the love of
the food one ate as a child?'

Lin Yutang, 1895–1976

introduction

Sue Lawrence, food writer
born 1955

One of my earliest memories involving food was New Year. Because we lived in Edinburgh, we used to drive to Dundee on New Year's Day (having checked the ferry times over the River Forth – this was pre-Forth Road Bridge) and undertake a 'royal tour'. There were so many relatives to visit: for Dad to have his dram, Mum her sherry and my sister Carol and me our blackcurrant cordial. I remember in particular visiting Great Auntie Maggie at number 12 Baxter Park Terrace, in a tenement block just beside where my dad was brought up at number 10. Her flat was on the first floor and I remember being amazed that there was no bedroom, the bed being a part of the sitting room overlooking the park; the back room, overlooking the green, had the tiniest of sculleries off it, the size of a large cupboard.

I must have been about three when I first remember sipping cordial from a tiny glass and eating shortbread or sultana cake, both served with a wedge of cheese. The New Year visits would continue all day: I recall Auntie May in the 1960s having a 'Party Susan', serving cubes of cheese and pineapple, pickled onions and other nibbles; Granny Ward always bought delicious Toffee Cups especially for my sister and me. The day would end up at Granny Anderson's for steak pie and mashed potatoes and then the grand finale: cloutie dumpling with silver threepennies in it.

There is another Dundee scene ingrained on my memory which, rather improbably, unites Charles Dickens and Marcel Proust. It was teatime at Granny Anderson's house. Around the table were twinsetted aunts and freshly scrubbed cousins; tea was moving on apace – from steak pie to pudding – and with the ice cream, which Uncle Frank ran to the Italian ice-cream shop to buy (no freezers), were Tunnock's Snowballs.

I can still remember biting through the coconut-studded chocolate shell into the gloriously sticky, snow-white goo within. I can also remember the sudden silence that fell upon the erstwhile Hovis-like scene when I said loudly, mouth still full, 'Can I have another Snowball?' Not, 'Please may I have some more?', as Oliver Twist might have said, or merely retained a silent longing as Marcel Proust did for page upon page.

So, when my wonderful yet formidable granny asked me, from the other end of the table, to repeat my request, the entire family stared. My Pollyanna politeness had temporarily departed with my greedy desire for another Snowball and it was only when my cousin David whispered to me, 'You've forgotten to say "please",' that I was able to breathe and remember my manners.

Back in Eskbank, outside Edinburgh, where we lived, I remember being at school, in Primary 1 and so proud of my wonderful red shoes – until a wasp somehow got inside them and stung my foot. I cannot remember the pain, only being rushed off to the Staff Room and being allowed to sit and eat as many digestive biscuits as I wanted from a large McVitie's biscuit tin, until my mum came to collect me and take me home.

I also remember wasps buzzing around the garden near the kitchen window when my mum was making preserves every summer – raspberry jam or blackcurrant jelly. Then my sister and I would sit on the draining board on either side of the big kitchen sink to wash our feet after a summer's day barefoot in the garden, and eat the jam still warm on Scotch pancakes, fresh from the girdle (griddle).

Later on, at Scripture Union Camp on Arran, where my friend Isabelle and I went each year from the age of twelve, wasps featured heavily. Although most years were so wet we had to abandon the tents and sleep on tables in the dining tent at the top of the field, one year there was a heatwave. And so, at each al fresco meal, we had to lay out Wasp Bait: a slice of bread spread thickly with jam and placed in the middle of the table. The wasps would alight and we would whack them violently with a spoon. By the end of the meal there were piles of jammy corpses, which seemed somehow incongruous given the purpose of the camp.

At lunch at Senior School, there was never any choice of meal. If it was a liver and onions day and you loathed liver, then, tough – and it usually was! Still, on roast potato day the queues formed early outside the lunch hall and the minute we sat down we picked up our forks and plunged them greedily into the biggest, crispiest roast potato in the bowl in the middle of the table. As Grace was being said, we clung onto the end of our forks for dear life, until we were allowed to pile up our plates. There were also repulsive dishes such as the lumpiest custard with the thickest skin imaginable, and what we charmingly referred to as YMCA (Yesterday's Muck Cooked Again): this was trifle.

Between the ages of seven and about fourteen, I spent most of my life outside my own home at the manse, where Isabelle lived. Mrs Doig's meatloaf and her chocolate pudding were divine, and it was there I would have my first taste of such un-Scottish dishes as boiled rice with chicken – a legacy of their years spent in Africa. I was usually asked to stay for tea and always accepted, gobbling down as much as I could before politely thanking Mrs Doig and leaving, only to run up the road – a good half mile – to my own home where I never told my mum about the manse tea, but simply sat down to a second tea. It was at one of Isabelle's birthday parties that I recall challenging her big brother Peter to a food race. I remember sitting in the dining room with him, both of us eating more and more sandwiches and cakes and trifle until at last I surrendered; he beat me by one Ritz cracker!

Nowadays, when looking through my mum's old recipe jotters with scribbled scraps of paper and pages torn out of magazines, I become nostalgic. Titles that leap out at me are those recipes I loved. From Mum's jotters, her sultana cake, cheese pudding, 'macaroni AND cheese', treacle scones, guggy cake, Border tart, and one of her later treats: ginger torte. From school days there are torn-out pages, probably from arithmetic jotters, with 'Baked Macaroni' topped with potato crisps, 'Toffee Cake' involving two threepenny bars of Highland Toffee, and 'Triple Decker Squares' (the old name for millionaire's shortbread). There is a recipe scribbled by a school chum for 'Chewy Stuff' (marshmallows, toffee, margarine, Rice Krispies) which asks me at the end 'Do you have a recipe for coconut balls?' (Luckily, four decades on, I do; if only I knew who had wanted it!) I recognise my sister's neat handwriting for 'Cheese and Sardine Tricorns', Mrs Hamilton's recipe for chocolate fudge, and Mrs Marshall's coffee buns.

With just one look at these smudgy pages I am transported back to my childhood and recall not only the taste and sight of the recipe (usually sweet), but also the provenance. And that is the wonderful thing about asking people about their childhood food memories. At the interviews for this book, I have encountered sadness, deep nostalgia, even tears on recalling something a mum or granny used to make. I have also witnessed laughter, disdain and passion. But most of all I have seen an enthusiasm about the food my interviewees ate as children and teenagers. On the whole, it was home-cooked, fresh and seasonal: how could that not evoke a delicious nostalgia? I spent many months interviewing the prominent Scots in this book and am hugely grateful to them for their time – and their recipes! Most of the dishes appear as told to me by the interviewees but if they didn't have one to hand, I have suggested a recipe of my own.

Hopefully by trying some of these dishes and reading the accompanying tales, you too can recall your own childhood food memories and so forge that link to the past that Proust wrote about, but instead of Madeleines, think mince, broth or shortbread. Taste the memory...

Guggy Cake
makes 1 loaf

This delicious, moist cake is based on one from my mum's regular teatime repertoire. I still have her original recipe, torn from a magazine from 1963, which used only cups for measurements and lard instead of butter.

150g/5½ oz light muscovado sugar
150g/5½ oz sultanas
150g/5½ oz currants
125g/4½ oz butter

2 tsp mixed spice
225g/8 oz self-raising flour
pinch of salt
butter, for greasing

Place the first 5 ingredients in a heavy saucepan with 250ml/9 fl oz cold water. Heat gently until the butter is melted, then remove from the heat and cool.

Once cold, sift in the flour and a pinch of salt and combine well. Tip into a buttered, base-lined, 1kg/2 lb 4 oz loaf tin, levelling the surface, and bake in an oven preheated to 180°C/350°F/Gas 4 for about 1 hour or until a skewer inserted into the middle comes out clean. Remove to a wire rack to cool before turning out.

Serve sliced, spread with butter.

soups and
starters

Kirsty Young, broadcaster
born 1968

Kirsty Young's first food memory was connected to her being naughty: her mother had just put a dish of rice pudding onto the kitchen table to cool then gone away. 'I went up with a spoon and took two huge spoonfuls, then tried madly to cover up the indentations, flattening the top over so no-one would know I had taken any!' She still loves rice pudding to this day.

Kirsty's grandmothers were both good cooks. Her paternal granny, Jessie Young, was 'an unbelievable baker', making wonderful shortbread and tablet but also the best birthday cakes, topped with royal icing. She also made lots of jams and pale jellies, often using berries collected by Kirsty.

'My other grandmother, Annie Allan, was not a fancy cook, but she made good, simple food such as potato soup and fried fish. Her apple pie was also delicious – more what we would call *tarte aux pommes* nowadays, but without a lid! When my mum asked her for the recipe she tried it and it didn't work. It was probably because Granny had to make something from nothing – she had to feed five children and a husband on very little – and so when she said to Mum to use one large apple, she probably used all the bits we would throw in the bin too!'

Kirsty's favourite childhood dishes are many, but she particularly likes Scottish plain bread and potato scones. When she returns to Scotland her mum cooks her a proper breakfast with home-made potato scones and black pudding, which she loves. Kirsty remembers the thrill of going out to a restaurant for her sister's birthday when they were children and having gammon and pineapple – which at the time was very 'modern'. She also fondly recalls her mum's pineapple upside-down cake. At Christmas her granny would serve smoked salmon first, which Kirsty came to adore, even though this seemed to her a very unusual taste. Another strange taste she recalls vividly was the combination of mushy peas with vinegar and a milkshake – served at a seaside café in Millport. This was where the family used to go on holiday from East Kilbride (where Kirsty lived until she was seven), and then from Stirling, her subsequent home.

Kirsty remembers her mother's cooking being pretty healthy – nothing fried, only grilled – though they were allowed the occasional treat of a fish supper when on holiday. Her mum's lasagne, she thought, 'was simply sophistication beyond my wildest dreams; I still crave that and Mum makes it for me when I am home'.

And as for childhood dislikes: 'We were never allowed to be fussy, we just ate everything! Though I do remember the most revolting combination at school dinners of watery mashed potatoes with Spam and baked beans.'

Kirsty learned to cook when she was seventeen, while working as an au pair, but her love for all things to do with food had started much earlier. At thirteen she began cutting out food reviews from the papers, such as Loyd Grossman from *Harpers & Queen* magazine, and she bought her first cookery book in Glasgow when aged twenty. 'It was a perfect choice for my first cookbook, really – *An Omelette and a Glass of Wine*, by Elizabeth David!'

Nowadays Kirsty likes to cook Scottish dishes such as soups (Scotch broth like her mum's) or steak pie or haggis. 'But if I want to cook haggis at home, that has to be when my husband is out as he does not like it at all.'

Memories of her Granny Allan's cloutie dumpling make Kirsty very nostalgic: 'It was so delicious, it was almost beyond belief. And when First Footing at Hogmanay, I loved the shortbread – and I was allowed a snowball (Advocaat and lemonade) if I was really lucky!'

Lentil and Ham Hock Soup
serves 4–6

approx. 175g/6 oz red lentils
soup stock made from a ham hock
    (or another tasty stock will do – but
    you would need to add chopped bacon
    to it), reserving some flecks of meat
25g–55g/1–2 oz butter
3 carrots, peeled and chopped

1 onion (or 1 chopped leek), peeled
    and chopped
1 medium potato (if the stock is
    over-salty), peeled and chopped
a handful of fresh parsley leaves,
    chopped

Add the lentils to the stock in a large saucepan and cook until thoroughly tenderised.

In the meantime, melt the butter in another saucepan and gently sauté the carrots, onion (or leek) and potato (if required). Add all these vegetables to the ham and lentil stock and simmer until you have a delicious soup.

Add the chopped parsley and some flecks of meat from the ham hock, then serve with a nice stick of French bread. Some people liquidise this soup to a thick creamy consistency before serving, but I never do this as I much prefer the look and taste as it is.

Sandy Lyle, golfer
born 1958

Sandy Lyle remembers stovies with great fondness, but his first real food memory was of a bowl of lentil soup, and being allowed to eat the ham off the shank as a treat. This soup became one of his favourite dishes as a child, and indeed he still loves a good bowl of it now: 'Especially during the cold winter days when you just can't beat a nice warming bowl of soup.'

One dish he remembers loathing as a child was tripe, for both 'its disgusting smell and texture'. However, his mum was a good baker as her sisters had their own little bakery shop in Milngavie, just outside Glasgow, and so she always made sure the family could enjoy some home baking: scones, shortbread (millionaire's) or pancakes.

The family never ate out much, although as Sandy got older they might go out for a Chinese or an Indian meal. Of his early visits to golf courses he recalls, 'On special outings we would go to the hotel restaurant at the golf course, which we also did at Christmas time. I hated it, because I'd rather have stayed home to play with my presents!'

Nowadays, Sandy can get by with cooking and is good at grilling – anything from a steak to asparagus – on the barbecue. 'But as for cooking special dishes, I will have to leave that to my dear wife. We still enjoy a fair bit of home baking, made by our trusty right and left hand, Carol, who is from Dunbar and helps look after the children; she has the touch and the patience!'

As for cooking Scottish dishes himself at home, 'Well, if you can call it cooking, maybe sticking some haggis in the microwave – and boiling and mashing the veggies! In our household I am more known for the Full Monty breakfast, with any style of eggs from our own hens.'

On trips back to Scotland, Sandy loves to eat 'anything that is tasty! First port of call will be the curry house. And, for home cooking, I love to get anything out of the Aga that has been slowly cooked, with lots of flavour. The kids and I love a mean Thai and luckily Jolande, my wife, has that down to a fine art. The rice cooker is probably our most-used kitchen gadget.'

Spicy Lentil Soup
serves 6–8

This is an adaptation of my mum's original lentil soup. If you don't have lentils, just add some chickpeas or a couple of potatoes to thicken it a bit. If you spot some Dutch smoked sausage, cut it into little cubes and add it to your bowl, either at the table or just before serving. And don't forget the bread for dunking!

butter
2 onions, peeled and chopped
some crushed dried chillies
a few black peppercorns, whole
a little brown sugar, to taste

2–3 bay leaves
1 ham hock
a couple of handfuls of red lentils
3–4 carrots, peeled and chopped
salt and pepper

Start by making the stock. Brown the chopped onions in a little butter in a large, ovenproof casserole, add the crushed chillies, the peppercorns, brown sugar, bay leaves and the hock. Cover with water, bring to the boil and put the casserole into the simmering oven of the Aga (or about 150°C/300°F/Gas 2 in a normal oven).

Once you think you have a nice-smelling and tasty stock, take out the hock and bay leaves, discarding the bay leaves. Add the lentils and carrots and stick it back in the oven.

In the meantime, pull the ham off the bone, ready to go back into the soup. (I like to keep some aside as it tastes great on some home-made soda bread.)

When the lentils and carrots are soft, blend, season to taste, add the ham, and you are good to go.

Nicola Sturgeon,
Deputy First Minister of Scotland
born 1970

Growing up in Irvine, in North Ayrshire, Nicola Sturgeon's earliest childhood food memories were, like those of so many other Scots, of her mum's mince and potatoes. 'We ate out only very occasionally, my favourite restaurant was a sit-in fish and chip shop in Prestwick, where I had the classic fish supper.'

Her gran was a great cook, and Nicola loved her Sunday roast with Yorkshire puddings. She also fondly remembers steak pie on New Year's Day, again cooked by her gran. One dish she hated was liver: 'I didn't like the taste of liver or even the thought of it!'

Nowadays there are certain childhood dishes that she still craves: 'I love sausages and mash, a great favourite from when I was small; you can't beat it for comfort food!' Nicola admits to being a terrible cook, but says she can turn her hand to soup – 'Vegetable soup is my only speciality' – and lentil soup is one of her regular dishes.

Bacon, Lentil and Kale Soup
serves 6

Sue says: This is my soup, made especially for Nicola. I like a sprinkling of grated Mull Cheddar on top too.

1 tbsp olive oil
5–6 rashers smoked streaky bacon,
    chopped
2 carrots, peeled and chopped
4 sticks celery, chopped
1 onion, peeled and chopped
150g/5½ oz dried green lentils
    (the no-soak variety)

225g can chopped tomatoes
1.7 litres/3 pints ham stock
150g/5½ oz washed and shredded
    kale (this is the prepared weight)
salt and pepper, to taste

Heat the oil in a large pan and sauté the bacon for a few minutes. Add the carrots, celery and onion. Continue to sauté for a few minutes.

Wash and drain the lentils then add to the pan with the tomatoes and stock. Bring to the boil then simmer for about 35–40 minutes. Add the kale and continue to cook for a further 10–15 minutes or until the kale is tender. Add some boiling water if it is too thick. Season to taste with salt and pepper before serving.

Aggie MacKenzie, TV presenter
born 1955

Aggie vividly remembers summers growing up in Rothiemurchus, in the Cairngorms. She used to sit on the back step with her sisters, clutching a bowl of white granulated sugar and dipping sticks of rhubarb from the garden into the sugar before crunching. 'I reckon this pastime is not unconnected to my mouthful of fillings,' she says.

Food was hugely important in Aggie's house. Both parents had been brought up in hardworking farming and crofting families, where you needed to eat proper food to provide enough energy for the work on the land. Everything was made from scratch and was tasty and wholesome. A week's meals might consist of roast beef on Sunday, cold roast on Monday, mince and tatties or stew and dumplings on Tuesday, fish on Wednesday from the travelling fishman (always haddock or herrings to be fried in oatmeal – never cod), then broth on Thursday with the boiled beef and mashed neeps and tatties in the same soup plate for the second course. 'Second day's broth' was then served on Friday, and perhaps chicken on Saturday. Aggie's sister Christine hated this soup, but they all remember their granny (who lived in Sutherland) making the best broth ever. Aggie's mum agreed, and once she even took back water from Sutherland to try to replicate the recipe, but even so the four MacKenzie sisters still didn't think it matched Granny's.

Apart from Granny's broth, Aggie's favourite meals included soused herring, cod's roe in butter, stew and dough balls (which even now she can make perfectly, provided her mum is standing by, otherwise she says they are chewy, dense and heavy). Another vivid childhood memory is racing back from primary school: 'I always tried to beat my sisters and be first home for lunch as the prize was a great treat – getting to suck the marrow bone from the soup pan.'

In winter the shed was – and still is – used for boiling the plum puddings (to avoid a steamy kitchen), and in summer her mum's blackcurrant jelly dripped away through the jelly bag over an upturned stool into a bowl. The cake tins were always filled with her mum's classic bakes, ever ready for visitors – whether expected or not. These treats included chocolate sandwich cake with chocolate butter cream, lemon drizzle cake, shortbread, gingerbread, millionaire's shortbread, and sometimes her Auntie Hughag's melting moments. Aggie recalls the bowl of butter and sugar laid by the fire every Friday (baking day), to soften a little before being mixed and baked.

Aggie's dad's siblings, Jock, Donald and Jessie, lived nearby. Between them they kept cows, sheep, pigs and hens and supplied Aggie's family with milk, cream and eggs. And although Aggie loathes milk puddings (sago, tapioca, semolina), a favourite was a 'jelly fluff'. Instead of being made with tinned Carnation milk, the half-set jelly was whipped with fresh cream. Divine. Auntie Jessie often used to eat a supper of tatties and milk, a sight that would make Aggie's stomach turn, but Jessie also cured her own bacon, and Aggie remembers the amazing flavour and the thickness of the slices, compared with today's meagre rashers.

When she goes home to Rothiemurchus, Aggie's mum always has a batch of scones freshly baked for her arrival off the train at 7.30am. She will also cook a selection of comforting dishes for her, such as stew, mince and lentil soup, during her visit.

Nowadays, London-based Aggie often makes mince and tatties for her family, as well as the famous broth. Here is Aggie's mum's recipe for Scotch broth, which she says is delicious on day one, two or even three.

Scotch Broth
serves 6

The beef is cooked to flavour the stock, then it should be removed before serving.

350g/12 oz piece marrow bone
1.4kg/3 lb 2 oz piece beef skirt
300ml/10 fl oz broth mix
2 medium carrots, peeled and finely
    chopped
2 medium onions, peeled and finely
    chopped

1 medium parsnip, finely chopped
¼ white cabbage, finely chopped
1 leek, finely chopped
1–2 level tbsp salt
2 level tbsp freshly chopped parsley,
    to serve

Put the marrow bone and beef skirt into a large saucepan and add 2.6 litres/4½ pints cold water (or enough to cover the meat). Bring to the boil, remove any scum and discard. Turn the heat down low, add the broth mix and simmer, partly covered, for 1½ hours, skimming the surface occasionally.

Add the carrots, onions, parsnip, cabbage and leek and another 600ml/1 pint water to the pan, cover to bring to the boil quickly, then simmer for another 30 minutes.

Remove the bone and beef from the soup. Season with salt and pepper, stir in the chopped parsley, and serve.

Ian Rankin, novelist
born 1960

Apart from fond memories of Farley's rusks in hot milk, some of Ian Rankin's earliest food memories are of his mum's Yorkshire puddings; she was from Bradford so knew how to make them the traditional way. These were served with gravy and roast silverside for Sunday lunch, unless it was roast chicken; for, as Ian recalls, there was a routine to the meals: 'Friday was fish, Saturday gammon steaks (with pineapple rings!), Sunday a roast – and that was after the Sunday morning fry-up of bacon, sausage and egg, which was after the routine Sunday morning dose of syrup of figs!'

Growing up in Cardenden, in Fife (where he lived until he was eighteen), there were lots of vans – butchers, fruit and veg, bakers – all delivering to the door, and so his mum, like everyone else, made fresh food every day. Soups were very big in his home; perhaps vegetable soup or chicken with rice. His mum also made the most wonderful jam tart: a home-made, thin pastry crust filled with home-made jam (usually raspberry) with a pastry lattice on top. This, served with custard, is one of Ian's favourite childhood puddings, along with oven-baked rice pudding. And as for savoury, it has to be mince and tatties, as 'no-one makes it quite like my mum did: quite thick so it all stuck together and served with marrowfat peas. Sometimes I had to go to my auntie's for lunch from primary school and I hated her mince as it was all watery; she also made tapioca pudding which I loathed, although I love semolina pudding with jam.'

Ian's dad ran the grocer's shop in Lochgelly, Fife, and so often brought home interesting goodies for the family. 'There were a lot of broken biscuits he would arrive home with and best of all was a big box of Jacob's Club biscuits.'

Some of the things his mum and dad enjoyed, such as bread with dripping, boiled tongue or – worst of all – potted '*heid*' (hough), he detested. But he did enjoy the potatoes his dad grew in the garden (boiled with a roast, mashed with mince) and also the home-grown rhubarb (washed then the raw sticks dipped in white sugar). But he also loved – then and now – properly made porridge. His was taken with sugar (now he prefers honey), his dad's with only salt. His abiding memory is that all food was seasonal: lettuce was only eaten in summer, as that was when his father grew it.

The chip shop in Cardenden was run by a man called Mr Curati, but Ian and his chums always thought his name was Joe Karate. 'We were all convinced he would spit into the fat to check if it was hot enough to fry the fish.' By the time Ian left Cardenden, in 1978, there was also one Chinese takeaway, but the one time his sister insisted the family go to a Chinese restaurant in St Andrews they all chose steak and chips! Ian never ate pasta, or rice, or pizza until he went to Edinburgh University at eighteen; and only then did he begin to eat cheese – because his flatmate used to eat it.

Ian can remember New Year at Cardenden with everyone out 'scrubbing their front steps and tidying the house on Hogmanay, to ensure it would be clean and tidy all year'. He also remembers the Hogmanay tables groaning with Black Bun, Battenburg cakes, shortbread – and the hot dish always being stovies, made with dripping, to soak up the alcohol. Although some stovies have the addition of corned beef, Ian's family's only had proper beef stirred in. Fray Bentos tinned corned beef was, however, a real treat, sliced very thickly. Another tinned treat he adored was Heinz Treacle Sponge Pudding, heated up then served with custard.

Nowadays, though, the evocative childhood dish he is most likely to cook is his mum's vegetable soup, which has become a great favourite in his own family.

Vegetable Soup
serves 4

1 onion
sunflower oil, for frying
garlic paste (optional)
2 leeks
3 potatoes

2 carrots
½ cabbage
½ turnip (swede)
Knorr liquid stock, to taste
dried mixed herbs

Chop and fry an onion in sunflower oil in a large saucepan, adding some garlic paste, if you like. Peel and dice the other vegetables, add to the pan and stir well. Cook them gently then chuck in enough boiling water to cover and some Knorr liquid stock (I like the vegetable stock) and some dried mixed herbs. I do not add any salt.

Simmer for 20–30 minutes, then, if this is for my sons Jack and Kit, I blend it so that the elder son Jack doesn't know he is eating vegetables (he only likes peas, cucumber and lettuce!), or otherwise I like it chunky. My wife Miranda and I eat it with good wholemeal bread, the boys with white bread to dunk.

David Coulthard,
Formula One racing driver
born 1971

David Coulthard's earliest childhood food memory was one that is familiar to so many of us: 'It was ice cream and jellies at parties.'

Food was important when he was growing up in Kirkcudbrightshire in the 1970s. His mum was always cooking and made fantastic soup; indeed, his favourite childhood dishes are still his mum's soups. Another great memory was of a full Scottish breakfast on a Sunday.

As a family, eating out was not a regular pastime, as there was not much choice of restaurants in rural Scotland; but they did go out for bar snacks.

David hated vegetables: 'Because my mother steamed them (the healthy option, I now realise), they were very hard. Today, though, I love them.' Now when David returns to Scotland he loves to eat 'anything fresh'.

Tattie Soup
serves 4

Sue says: This is my tattie soup recipe, one of David's favourites.

1.2 litres/2 pints good chicken stock
1kg/2 lb 4 oz potatoes, peeled
1 large onion, peeled

3–4 carrots, peeled
salt and pepper, to taste
chopped fresh chives or parsley
        leaves, to garnish

Bring the stock to the boil in a large saucepan.

Chop the vegetables into similarly sized dice and add to the pan, along with some salt and pepper. Cover and cook over a medium heat for 25–30 minutes until the vegetables are all tender. Taste and check the seasoning.

Ladle the soup into bowls and sprinkle each bowl with some chives or parsley.

Shirley Spear, chef
born 1952

One of Shirley Spear's first memories is of sitting in a pram seat, her brother in the pram and being taken to the clinic for tins of baby milk and bottles of orange juice with a blue cap. She also recalls being given a tablespoon of malt from a big brown jar and a daily dose of rosehip syrup. Shirley told me how she collected rosehips when she was at primary school and was given six pence a pound for them (presumably to make the syrup). I too recall this early form of child labour!

Food was important in Shirley's house when she was growing up, but since there were five children it was always good but simple fare. Shirley remembers helping her mum roll out pastry for jam tarts and her mum insisting on putting her – by now grey – pastry cases on the garden fence for the birds to eat instead of the family! There was always lots of home baking going on when she lived in Peebles (where they lived until she was eight, before they moved to Edinburgh), as people were always popping in for a cup of tea. There would be shortbread, fairy cakes, Victoria sponge, and for special occasions or parties they would make 'chocolate truffles' from porridge oats, coconut and cocoa mixed with melted margarine and syrup, formed into balls then rolled in coconut. 'Mum's meringues were also really good, nicely gooey in the middle. We would fill them with tinned Nestlé cream.'

Daily meals would consist of mince, liver and onions, fish in Ruskoline, Lorne sausage with fried egg and slow-cooked stews. 'I've inherited from my mum the love of making stews and casseroles,' says Shirley, 'and though I also adore making soups now, she didn't make them often. We would always have a family Sunday roast – beef with horseradish or sometimes mutton, always with roast potatoes. And there was often tinned fruit salad and we would all end up arguing over the cherry from the tin! Mum's rice pudding was also wonderful, with a lovely, brown, nutmeggy skin.'

At the end of their road in Peebles, a few doors down from their house, lived two spinster sisters and their brother, who was a shepherd. Sometimes young Shirley would wander into their house around lunchtime as she was fascinated by the daily ritual: the brother would arrive home from the farm, sit on the stairs to remove his boots, then at the table his sisters would serve him an entire shepherd's pie in an oblong enamel tin. 'He would eat the lot! And of course I thought – for many years in fact – that the pie was so-called because he was a shepherd! He always had Pan Drops in his pocket and I would always come home with some – much to Mum's horror, as she was concerned about the proximity of sweeties to dirty handkerchiefs!'

Hallowe'en is a festival that Shirley feels strongly about: 'I feel very sad about Hallowe'en, as it has been hijacked by the Americans, though in Scotland we have always celebrated it. I remember having to howk out a turnip, then use string for the handles and pop a candle inside. The smell of the burnt raw turnip is an abiding memory. We often had Hallowe'en parties at home and we would make papier mâché witches as decoration and I would help Mum make toffee apples. There would be tablet and treacle scones and we would dook for apples. I remember once going guysing dressed as one of three highwaymen with my two chums. We had my brother's cowboy gun with us and I had bought some penny caps to fire, and we ended our song and dance routine at the doors with a shot of the gun and a cry of "Your money or your life", which horrified my mother as we were not allowed to ask for money, as the kids nowadays seem to expect. One of my favourite ways of using the insides of a turnip after hours of turnip lantern-making, is in soup.'

Neep Bree

serves 6

Bree is an old Scottish word for a broth. This is a great lunchtime soup and perfect with some warm cheese scones, straight from the oven, on a cold day.

50g/1¾ oz butter
2 medium or large onions, peeled and
    chopped small
1 large neep (a yellow, swede turnip),
    peeled and diced small (weighing
    approx. 500g/1 lb 2 oz when
    prepared)
piece of whole root ginger, approx.
    the size of the top of your thumb,
    finely grated

salt and pepper, to taste
juice and finely grated rind of
    1 large orange
1 litre/1¾ pints vegetable stock
approx. 125ml/4 fl oz milk
125ml/4 fl oz double cream,
    to serve
finely chopped fresh chives,
    to garnish

Melt the butter in a large saucepan until foaming. Add the onions and cook until soft, but not brown. Stir in the turnip and mix well. Add the grated ginger, plus some salt and freshly ground black pepper. Put the lid on and allow the vegetables to cook gently for 5–10 minutes, stirring occasionally.

Pour in the orange juice and rind. Stir well. Add the stock, bring to boil and then reduce the heat and simmer slowly, with the lid on, for 1 hour.

Add the milk and liquidise thoroughly. (The soup can be cooled and frozen at this stage.) Check the seasoning to taste and stir the cream through. Heat thoroughly before serving. (If too thick, add a little more milk or cream, especially if reheating from cold.)

Serve with a sprinkling of finely chopped chives and some warm cheese scones.

Wholemeal Cheese Scones
makes 12

When we first opened The Three Chimneys on Skye, I served these scones with home-made soup at lunchtimes. We still have customers who remember driving all the way to us to enjoy a bowl of neep bree with warm cheese scones – especially on a cold, Skye day! They are best served soon after they are baked, but they also freeze well.

100g/3½ oz wholemeal self-raising flour
100g/3½ oz white self-raising flour
½ tsp table salt
½ tsp mustard powder
¼ tsp cayenne pepper
1 scant level tsp bicarbonate of soda

40g/1½ oz Scottish butter, diced
200g/7 oz mature white Scottish Cheddar cheese, finely grated
1 large free-range egg
approx. 75–100ml/2½–3½ fl oz fresh milk

Sift the flours together with the salt, mustard powder, cayenne and bicarbonate of soda. Rub in the butter to the dry ingredients, using the tips of your fingers. Add the grated cheese and mix together lightly with your fingers.

Beat the egg and 75ml/2½ fl oz of the milk together, add to the mixture and bind to make a smooth dough, using the rounded blade of a table knife. Add more milk if necessary.

Using your hands, gently pull the dough together in the mixing bowl to form a smooth ball, adding a little more milk if the mixture seems too dry. Place the dough on a floured board and roll it out evenly to a thickness of 4cm/1½ in – no thinner. Cut out the scones with a 5cm/2 in straight-sided cutter, pushing down into the dough without twisting it. This helps to make the scones rise evenly.

Place the scones on a floured baking tray and lightly brush the tops of each with a little more milk. Finally, sprinkle the remaining grated cheese on the top of each scone.

Bake on the centre shelf of an oven preheated to 220°C/425°F/Gas 7, for 12–15 minutes or until risen and golden.

Remove to a cooling tray. Resist eating until you are ready to serve!

Alex Salmond,
Scotland's First Minister
born 1954

Alex Salmond remembers 'winding' molten tablet round a wooden spoon in the kitchen of his Linlithgow home as a toddler. He also recalls, when he was slightly older, being allowed to stir the bubbling mass in the pan. Made from Carnation milk because of his severe allergy to cow's milk (for some reason Carnation milk was acceptable), he smiled at the memory of his mother's tablet: 'No-one makes it like that now.'

His was a house of all-home cooking, without any convenience foods. His mum was an excellent cook and baker, as was his grandmother. His aunt worked in Oliphant's, the baker's in Linlithgow, and so had no need to bake at home. This was the shop where, Alex told me, 'they made the best muffins in Scotland. The queues every Saturday went on for ever.'

But it was his mother's Christmas cakes that were the talk of the town. 'She would make some fifty each year, to give out to extended family, friends and "old folk". I used to dispatch them. My Great Auntie Aggie's birthday was New Year's Day and I remember going to her house with her cake in particular. My birthday is on Hogmanay, and so in our family we had two days of ongoing celebrations!' Alex describes his mother's cakes very fondly: 'These were serious cakes. I remember the packets of dried fruit all over the kitchen and then, once they were all done – some were iced, some left for the recipient to ice – they were foil-wrapped before being sent out. They lasted for ages. Indeed, though my mother died in 2003, we kept one of her cakes and still enjoyed it, albeit with a slight hint of sadness and nostalgia, three or four years later.'

As well as the myriad cakes he had to help distribute, Alex's mother's Christmas puddings were also legendary, but these were made only for the immediate family. They used to ignite them with brandy on Christmas Day and he vividly recalls the flames: 'On more than one occasion, they seemed to set everything alight, not just the pudding!'

One of Alex's favourite childhood dishes was rice pudding, which he adored – skin and all. Of course, it was not made with cow's milk but with goat's milk, on which he practically lived. Fortunately, there were goats nearby and their milk was specially delivered to the Salmond house. He also remembers wonderful picnics, perhaps into the Bathgate Hills and, in particular, the squashed tomato sandwiches: 'The bread got all squashed from the soft tomatoes – and the foil they were wrapped in somehow gave them a better taste!'

Sunday school picnics were also a huge treat, but he has never forgotten the traumatic picnic of 1963 when, all of eight years old, he didn't get his Lucky Bag. The teachers had simply forgotten to give him the special bag containing an apple, a bag of crisps, chocolate biscuit and a bar of McGowan's Highland toffee. His wistful look suggested to me that he still feels peeved that he was the only child not to receive the Lucky Bag all those years ago!

While growing up, Alex learned to cook very little – apart from that wonderful tablet – but at university he mastered most student dishes, such as spaghetti Bolognese, and sometimes he would even save up to buy steak, as it was so easy to cook. There was no food he loathed, apart from tinned spaghetti.

Alex took part in a recent campaign to promote Scottish food by eating only Scottish produce for a week, and he survived admirably. He shopped for everything himself and cooked it all; each meal costing no more than £1 a head.

Another Scottish dish Alex adores is steak pie ('My wife Moira makes a serious steak pie!'), but he also loves good Scottish butchers' pies, citing butchers in Aberdeen, Inverurie and Huntly as some of the best. His mother used to make steak pie for New Year's Day (followed by cloutie dumping or trifle), but also for The Marches. This is a centuries-old tradition that takes place in Linlithgow on the first Tuesday after the second Thursday in June. In the town it is still a very important event, and so steak pie, just as at New Year, was part of the celebration.

Cullen Skink

serves 4

Sue says: Alex's wife Moira got this recipe from the chef at the Pennan Inn on the Banffshire coast, but the word 'skink' brings back other memories for Alex, as his dad used to call him a skink as a child because he was so skinny!

2 medium smoked haddock fillets or
    1 large finnan haddock
2 medium onions, peeled and chopped
55g/2 oz butter, plus a knob for the mash

450g/1 lb potatoes, peeled
425ml/¾ pint milk
salt and pepper, to taste
chopped fresh parsley, to garnish

Place the fish in a pan with enough cold water to cover. Bring slowly to the boil and simmer for 10 minutes. Take out the fish, retaining the liquor, then remove and discard the bones and skin. Flake the fish.

In another pan, cook the onions in the butter.

Boil the potatoes in another pan, and when cooked, mash them with the knob of butter before adding the liquor from the fish, the milk and onion (and buttery juices). Add salt and pepper to taste, then serve in warm bowls with parsley scattered on top.

Bill Pryde, artist–printmaker
born 1951

Bill Pryde was brought up on Blackford Hill in Edinburgh by his grandmother, maiden great-aunt and guardian, since both his parents had died when he was very young. He therefore recalls his childhood as being in a time warp; more like 1930s Scotland, not the 1950s and 1960s. His grandmother used to regularly host large tea parties: 'It was her way of keeping control of the extended family,' says Bill. And as well as the etiquette involved, his abiding memory as a child was of the leftover sandwiches (egg and cress, ham and tomato) being fried for breakfast the next day. 'In fact, we used to beg her to make sandwiches at night just to have the next day for breakfast, they were so delicious.'

At these teas there would also be sausage rolls – made with his grandmother's wonderful home-made pastry – and cakes such as chocolate and Victoria sponge, and little orange jellies studded with tinned mandarin oranges (these latter not only for the children, but for the old ladies, too).

Bill also recalls visits to Lucas ice-cream shop after a day at Portobello beach with the magnificent wooden wave-machine; and also 'what was the height of sophistication, Orange Jubblies: pyramid-shaped, solid ice lollies that you would slowly remove the wrapper from as you sucked it, juice-like at first and then, miraculously, it transformed into orange sorbet. I loved these!'

Soup was a hugely important part of his childhood, being eaten twice a day. 'I am a soup fanatic now and make it often, even though I had the same type – ham and lentil – every single day as a child! I also make cullen skink and often serve it chilled in summer, which is delicious. And I put garlic into my own ham and lentil soup, which was never even mentioned in genteel Edinburgh of the early 1960s. Similarly, fish and chips were never allowed in the house; the only time we had them was on visits to North Berwick and we could go to the chip shop after a bracing swim in the outdoor pool.'

Bill has never had a sweet tooth, and so the best school dinner of the week was fish and chips on a Friday – he savoured every morsel. Since he took his time with this fabulous dish, everyone else would have finished and pudding was served while he was still eating his fish.

However, the sight of a bowl of frogspawn (tapioca) with a dollop of tinned strawberry jam thumped down in front of him made him ill. Almost every Friday he would be sick, as he so loathed puddings.

Eating out when he was a child was not usual, but he does remember being taken, with his brother, to the Braid Hills Hotel on occasion for lunch. 'The "starter" was always a choice of juices – pineapple, grapefruit or tomato – or, if you were very lucky, the choice included grapefruit segments.' Because the family had Hong Kong connections, they also used to go to Morningside's one and only Chinese restaurant every now and again, and he recalls his grandmother and all the ladies dressing up in hats, silk scarves and finery as if going to a formal dinner! Bill's grandmother 'invented' curried baked beans: she would stir curry powder into tinned baked beans and heat them up – long before Heinz brought out their own version. His uncle also invented the coloured golf ball in the early 1960s (a blue one, to be seen in the snow), but forgot to patent it: something the family now agree was more than a little foolish!

Later on, as a student, Bill was able to cook the basics – such as a roast chicken – if only just to impress a date, but his best student dish was eggs poached in a pan of Heinz tomato soup. He still makes this delicacy now and loves it. Whenever Bill returns to Edinburgh for an exhibition or to visit friends, he gets off the train at Waverley station and, wheelie-bag in tow, goes to the first baker or butcher for a proper Scotch pie, as these are something he misses so much when he is down south.

Overall, Bill remembers food as a child as healthy ('we had cabbage with everything') but very routine. When he was ill, it was a treat to be in bed and be brought his grandmother's famous invalid's soup – which is still a favourite nowadays, whether feeling well or ill.

Invalid's Cullen Skink
serves 1

1 white fish fillet, such as haddock
milk
a knob of butter

salt and white pepper, to taste
1 tbsp yesterday's mashed potatoes
chopped fresh parsley, to garnish

Poach the fish in milk (enough to just cover it) and a knob of butter until just done. Add salt and white pepper to taste.

Stir in the mashed potatoes (enough to thicken once stirred through), then reheat gently. Serve in a warm bowl with plenty of parsley scattered on top.

Carol Smillie, broadcaster
born 1961

Carol Smillie's earliest food memory growing up in Glasgow was of eating a steak sandwich her mum had made for her to take on a school trip: 'I can still taste it now, it was so delicious,' she recalls.

Her mum did all the cooking, but, according to Carol, 'she was not a very adventurous cook, bless her. Nothing had any sauce or seasoning, and she could nuke a piece of meat to within an inch of its life!' A favourite childhood dish, though – and one she still craves – is good old mince and tatties: 'a firm favourite with my kids today.'

Carol's husband Alex is a restaurateur (he owns four restaurants in St Andrews and Stirling), so eating out is not unusual in her own family, but she never ate out as a child. Very occasionally the family had fish and chips on the way home from a day trip to the seaside, but, she says, 'we were a typical Presbyterian Scots bunch, which meant that to us, eating out was quite fancy'.

Carol hated most green vegetables as a child; indeed, even to this day, she says, 'I would sooner pull out my own fingernails than eat a Brussels sprout.'

She did a bit of baking with her mum, mostly simple stuff – scones, fairy cakes, etc – and her thirteen-year-old daughter is now a brilliant baker and really interested in food. Her birthday party last year was a cookery party where ten girls prepared a three-course dinner and then sat down to dinner to enjoy it... with Carol and husband Alex as the waiters. These are changed days from Carol's childhood parties: 'New Year's Day was always spent at my auntie's house with all my cousins and aunties and uncles. There were lots of roasts, trifles and home baking, and we ate in shifts as there were too many people. I remember the washing-up being fun as there was a great line of us all at it together!'

Nowadays Carol's own favourite dish at home is probably still a roast dinner, which the family always do on a Sunday, that is also ideal for making her mum's soup from the leftovers. If they are eating out, however, she loves fusion cooking – 'anything with coconut, ginger and coriander usually does it for me.'

Home-made Chicken Soup

serves 6

carcass of a roast chicken, or
chicken thighs, skin on
chicken stock, to cover

350g/12 oz/2 cups rice
a handful of chopped fresh parsley
salt and pepper, to taste

Place the carcass of a roast chicken or some chicken thighs with the skin on in a large saucepan and simmer in chicken stock for an hour or so. Then break up the chicken pieces (removing the bones and skin and returning any meat to the stock), cool the stock, then, once chilled, skim off any excess fat.

Return the stock to the boil, add the rice and the chopped parsley. Cook until the rice is tender. Season to taste and serve with fresh crusty bread and butter.

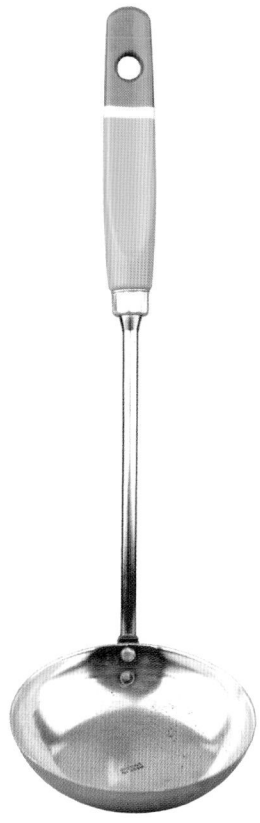

Sharleen Spiteri, singer
born 1967

Sharleen Spiteri told me her first food memory was toast and Marmite, which she loved, but then she remembered another great favourite of hers when she was about five or six years old: stuffed olives. This very un-Scottish childhood food gives an inkling of her not entirely Scottish roots. On her mother's side there was Scottish influence, but on her father's there was a strong Maltese heritage. Sharleen was aware that she was growing up with two very different culinary backgrounds.

As a family outing, when her dad was home from sea (he was a merchant seaman), they would go to Ferguson's the Deli on Union Street in Glasgow to buy olives, pâtés, anchovies and other delicacies which were almost unheard of in most Scottish households in the early 1970s. She also remembers the big boxes of broken biscuits from the large department stores' food halls in Glasgow. But apart from that, there was very little in the way of sweet things; unlike most Scots she did not have a sweet tooth and would still prefer a cheese platter to a dessert. The family never ate puddings, although they did always sit round the table, adults and children, in true Mediterranean style, to discuss everything that was going on. One sweet thing Sharleen did love, though, was tablet, and also her Aunt Marlene's baking.

Of other dishes eaten when she was growing up in Glasgow she told me, 'I never realised then that I had an educated palate from my parents, but I obviously did.' So from eating stew and dumplings and potted hough sandwiches regularly, she would also learn to cook 'kofta': minced beef combined with garlic, onion, red wine and egg, rolled into balls then grilled. These were served in Sharleen's house with home-made chips. 'Well, not really chips: my mum had a big mandoline slicer and she would cut the potatoes very fine then fry them in olive oil. We would also have a big salad on the table, dressed in good home-made vinaigrette which, after the salad was gone we would all dunk our bread into.'

She hated the whites of egg as a child – and still does – so she would eat a boiled egg but only the yolk with toast dippers. But she did like more unusual foods such as whelks: 'I remember having a bag of these at The Barras, with a pin to poke them out of the shell and then sometimes smearing the black bit onto my face as a beauty spot!'

When her dad was home, he would sometimes produce prawn cocktail for the family, making his own delicious cocktail sauce. When I asked Sharleen if this was for Christmas or New Year she said, 'No, we never ate anything different for special occasions as every day we ate well. Mum cooked everything from scratch and Dad sometimes cooked too, things like the prawn cocktail, but made such a mess, using every single pan in the house.'

Whenever she visits Scotland, Sharleen stocks up on 'a month's supply of tattie scones which I eat fried and with brown sauce – and tinned tomatoes heated in a pan'. Another favourite childhood dish was her mum's chicken and lemon soup, which was wonderfully tangy. When I suggested the lemons seemed unusual additions in a Scottish household, she told me there were always lemons in their kitchen. This wonderful soup sums up Sharleen's Scottish and Mediterranean heritage.

Chicken and Lemon Soup
serves 6

1 onion
1 carrot, finely diced
1 whole roast chicken
chicken stock, enough to cover generously

125g/4½ oz/¾ cup rice
1 lemon, plus extra to serve
1 egg

Chop then fry an onion in a large pan to soften it, then add the finely diced carrot. Once that's softened too, take a whole roast chicken, remove the flesh and add it to the pan. Then add loads of chicken stock and the rice, and boil it until done. Leave to cool a little until it's just warm.

Squeeze the juice of 1 lemon, whisk this together with the egg, then, very, very slowly stir this into the soup so it becomes creamy. The soup should now be a lovely pale yellow colour.

Place a couple of extra lemons on the table (to add a bit more juice to the soup if you want) and a loaf of crusty bread and serve the soup.

Janice Galloway, novelist
born 1955

Janice Galloway first recalls drinking Del Rosa rosehip syrup as a child and loving it. When, however, as a teenager she found an old bottle in a cupboard and tried it, she could hardly believe how awful it was! She also remembers having a sore throat and being given a ball of butter rolled in sugar; though she also had 'pieces with sugar' (white sugar sandwiches) when she was well. Where she grew up in Saltcoats, Ayrshire, there were two nearby ice-cream shops selling the best Italian–Scots ice cream imaginable. 'One of them was so good, it tasted like frozen tablet!

'Food was important in my house, but since my mother was a dinner lady she brought leftovers home, and these were always gratefully received, with the exception of the green blancmange. It tasted not unlike Angel Delight, but I never liked it. We got it because the kids hated it and so there was plenty left to bring home! Though my mum also used to hide a tray of caramel cake from the weans and bring that home, more surreptitiously. That was wonderful: shortcrust pastry base topped with boiled condensed milk and topped with dear old Scotbloc (chocolate covering).'

Although food was important at home, the cupboards were always full of chocolate biscuits – Clubs, Blue Ribands and KitKats. These latter were also breakfast. When I asked why, she explained: 'My mother was brought up on a frugal diet including daily porridge for breakfast (which I make now, though with luxury organic oats) and so wanted better for her own kids. So she reckoned KitKats were the thing; they were also perfect (not too heavy or sharp) to throw at us as we lay in bed: this was the sign we had to get up, eat the KitKat, then out to school in ten minutes!'

Home-made soup was always on the go: 'I am hard pushed to find a recipe from childhood that was not out of a tin or fresh from the school dinner hall, but there was always soup – lentil or chicken. We also ate steeped, then boiled-to-death, marrowfat peas with malt vinegar for a Friday night treat once a month or so. And we had "pat-a-cakes" – leftover beef, minced then mixed with mashed potatoes and plenty of salt and pepper, covered in Ruskoline and fried. These were served with pickled onions, which I also loved. Indeed, I often took to school a bottle of vinegar drained off from the large jar of silverskin pickled onions to drink. And later on, when I was a teenager, I would buy two large pickled onions to go with my fish supper (I also loved black pudding supper). Once it was finished, I would rub my hands all over the vinegary onions then wipe them on my boyfriend's coat to get rid of the greasiness!'

Janice still loves pickles of all types and often makes chutneys, either from green tomatoes or marrow (the latter having a good dod of whisky added, to bring out the flavour). She taught herself to cook when she thought that was what every teenage girl had to do, so when she won the music prize at school the teacher was horrified when she asked for a cookery book (a Marguerite Patten) as her prize.

Janice says she still makes pretty good Dundee cake, Black Bun, stovies, clapshot with haggis, macaroon bars (from mashed potatoes), tattie scones and shortbread. 'But I stopped making tablet as it is just far too easy to eat!'

And even though she loved eating chip-shop chips as a teenager, one of the few things she refused to eat at home (as well as green blancmange) was home-made chips. 'It was like a form of childhood rebellion, as my sister always ate them – potatoes freshly dug from the garden, peeled, chipped then fried in Cookeen that was used over and over. I used to watch the pile of chips dotted with burnt toast-crumb-like patches from the well-used fat. They turned my stomach!'

But, recalling her mum's wonderful soups, Janice's chicken soup recipe is not only comprehensive, it is also delicious.

Chicken Soup with Rice

serves 6

Chicken soup was Sunday fare, usually with a couple of slices of plain bread (from the cheapest wax-wrapped packet) for dipping, to bulk us up. Leftover chicken followed on Monday. I still make this.

For the stock:

1 whole, medium-sized, free-range
   chicken from a butcher
1 large onion, split in two
2–3 large, whole carrots
a couple of stalks of celery, whole

salt and pepper, to taste
bay leaves
some parsley stalks
   (retain the leaves for the soup)

Put the chicken (with the skin on, or it will fall to bits) in a big pot with the onion, carrots, celery, seasoning and herbs (plus whatever other little bits of flavouring you fancy). Barely cover the bird with water and bring to the boil. Once it's rolling, reduce the heat to a simmer and let it cook for around an hour and a half or until it looks as though the flesh is ready to fall away from the bones. Take it off the heat and remove the chicken right away. Let the water (now stock) cool, then sieve it to take out the veg and whatever fat has accumulated on top. Now you can use it to make lovely soup.

For the soup:

the cooked chicken
1 stick celery, chopped small
2–3 leeks, finely chopped
2 bay leaves
a knob of butter
salt and pepper, to taste

the stock
175g/6 oz/1 cup long-grain rice,
   washed under the tap
a big handful of chopped fresh parsley
a few chopped greentails (spring onions)

Shred all the chicken meat off the carcass and set aside.

In a large pot, add the celery, leeks and bay leaves to the butter and fry very lightly until they soften but do not brown (only a few minutes). Season this vegetable mixture with salt and pepper.

Pour in the sieved or skimmed stock (you might prefer to use only half or three-quarters of it if you want less soup) and gently bring it to the boil. Add the rice and simmer the whole lot for around 20 minutes at most.

Stir in as much shredded chicken as you fancy and season again to taste. Add the chopped parsley and greentails last, and serve with sliced bread and a lump of Ayrshire Dunlop cheese on the side.

veg, cheese and breakfast

BREAD

Gordon Ramsay, chef
born 1966

Gordon Ramsay's earliest memories of food involve great pots of ham hock and barley soup. 'I was probably between four and eight when I remember us all sitting down and eating this. It was so good; the ham from the bone was shredded back into the soup which was thick with barley. I also remember the horrible smell of tripe cooked in milk with onions; my dad loved tripe. I did not!'

When the family moved from Scotland to Stratford-upon-Avon, his mum worked in a tea shop called The Cobweb Tearooms. She would bring home any 'leftovers', and of these Gordon can remember bread and butter pudding, lemon meringue pie and strawberry sundaes. 'There were also those huge rectangular quiches that were just becoming popular back then. Mum also made really good rice pudding with milk, which I loved; and during the bread strikes she baked her own bread. She was a great cook. The food was humble, simple, but good; we were a family of six so she had to get home from work and cook for us all. And whether it was cabbage or sprouts, or a nice pudding, we just ate up, as we were hungry! We never left a thing on our plates. Tea was a time of great excitement, though, a joy; to drink, we always had a glass of milk.'

On Sundays the children would go to Sunday school, then the family would all sit down to a roast – almost always roast beef with roast potatoes. Gordon fondly remembers bubble and squeak made with the leftovers: 'Mum made it with the potatoes and cabbage and fried it in a large frying pan so it was like a big Spanish omelette.'

They occasionally had fish suppers and Gordon remembers also the unique 'delicacy' of saveloy suppers, the sausage being coated in batter and deep-fried.

Some of his favourite childhood dishes were sweet: his mum's home-made Bakewell tart was wonderful. 'And I loved Battenburg cake as a child, though that was always shop-bought. As well as Mum's rice pudding, I also loved rhubarb crumble served hot with custard.'

As for childhood hates, apart from tripe, Gordon was not keen at all on liver, as it was pig's liver which, when overcooked (as it always was at school), he thought was awful. Kidneys also were a problem, although these are now something he loves, but only if cooked rare.

Gordon never learned to cook at home as he was always too keen to get out and kick a football around, but now he loves to cook Scottish dishes such as cock-a-leekie soup with prunes, or bashed neeps. He has also taught his chefs to make haggis from scratch. And so, on visits north of the border, he loves to eat haggis; he also enjoys eating good Scottish salmon, as well as oysters and scallops from the West coast. Tattie scones are another treat that he loves to eat at breakfast, topped with a fried egg.

Most days before school, Gordon and his siblings would go swimming then return home for breakfast before school. This was invariably porridge, which he loved. But when the family moved to England, there was something called Ready Brek. Gordon hated this, as it was sloppy textured and had no substance, so they had packets of Scott's Porridge Oats sent down from Glasgow to Stratford-upon-Avon, and it was the beefy, caber-tossing Scottish male on the front of the packets that he aspired to. 'But then look what happened!' he laughs.

Porridge
serves 4

150g/5½ oz porridge oats or
    medium ground oatmeal
500ml/1 pint water

500ml/1 pint semi-skimmed milk
pinch of fine sea salt (optional)

To serve:
4 tbsp low-fat natural or Greek yoghurt
some runny honey or brown sugar, to taste
a handful of toasted flaked almonds

Put the oats, water, milk and salt, if using, into a medium saucepan. Stirring well, place over a high heat until the mixture begins to boil. Turn the heat down to low, stir frequently for 5–8 minutes as the porridge bubbles and thickens. Cook until it has the consistency you like, adding a splash of water if you prefer thinner porridge.

Remove from the heat, divide between warm bowls, top each with yoghurt, honey or sugar and a scattering of almonds. It is also good served with fresh fruit in season or dried fruit compote.

Bill Paterson, actor
born 1945

'I have a terrible memory of an egg – it might have been fried or boiled, but it was ghastly. I could only have been a toddler as I remember sitting in a wooden high chair. Ever since then I have never been able to be in the same building as a fried or boiled egg!' Bill Paterson's first childhood food memories are not good, but he has overcome some of his egg prejudices: 'From about the age of twenty I was able to eat an omelette or scrambled eggs, but never a fried or boiled egg!'

As Bill Paterson was growing up in his Dennistoun tenement in Glasgow, there was good food at home, his mum being 'a spectacular soup- and jam-maker'. She made chicken soup, lentil soup and Scotch broth. Every summer she made jams from fruits in season; blackcurrant, raspberry and strawberry jams were made from shop-bought fruit, but she would also make bramble jam from the berries Bill and his friends would pick for her. 'I remember the press in the front room always being well stocked: the entire bottom shelves were laden with jars of neatly labelled jam.'

His granny, who was from Lochaber, made tattie scones on her old-fashioned girdle, or griddle (the type made to hang over a fire). Bill also vividly remembers his Highland granny's favourite snack of oatcakes with Gorgonzola cheese, which must have been a bit of a rarity in 1940s Scotland!

His Auntie Polly, who ran a guest house in Dunoon, made wonderful ham and lentil soup, one of his favourite childhood dishes, along with cheese on toast, which he would make with his dad: they would spear bread and toast it in front of the fire then put the cheese on top (good Scottish Cheddar) and finish it off under the grill.

As well as eggs, Bill also hated milk puddings such as tapioca and rice puddings; custard, though, he liked – particularly when his mum stirred in some cocoa powder to make chocolate custard. He also loathed tripe and potted hough, the latter for its gelatinous texture.

He admits he was a faddy child and didn't enjoy eating at anyone else's house. If he was playing at a friend's house and was invited to stay for tea, he would make some excuse to get home. Bill's dad was a commercial traveller and would often eat out in hotels, and if Bill went with him, what might otherwise seem a luxury for a child was for him torture. He would always have the breaded fish, which he felt was safe.

Fish and chips, however, were a treat: they lived above a Scots–Italian café called the Swallow Café, whose fish and chips were very good. For one shilling and ten pence (about nine pence in new money) he could buy a delicious fish supper. Since, as well as the chip shop, there was also a butcher's shop beneath their tenement block, they would have steak pie, 'an ashet pie, delicious stewed beef underneath a crust and placed in the characteristic metallic dish, which we would return empty to the butcher, ready to be filled with our next steak pie.'

As a teenager, since he never took school dinners, Bill came home for lunch and used to make himself something with ham and tomato, and usually some chips. His mum would have peeled and cut the potatoes and left them in a bowl of cold water so that all he had to do was deep-fry them. Even though he was about fourteen, Bill reckons no working mum would even consider allowing a young son home alone these days to 'play' with boiling fat!

Nowadays he loves to cook herring in oatmeal, if he can find herring fillets. And he loves shortbread and tablet but finds it difficult not to finish the entire packet. Bill remembers going to church sales of work: 'The purpose of them for us was purely to get tablet. We used to go there only to get Mrs Cameron's or Mrs McFadgeon's tablet.'

Whenever he returns to Scotland from London, Bill loves eating kippers for breakfast: 'It's always good to eat them in a hotel as, easy though they are to do at home, the smell lingers and I get a row!' He also loves Lorne (square) sausage, which, when he is filming in Scotland, is the film crew's favourite, although, he says, 'Lorne sausage is wonderful, but only eat it if you can square it first with your cardiologist!'

But another favourite is tattie scones, which is how Bill uses leftover mashed potato, as he always makes far too much. 'For multi-cultural Scots, it also works with a combination of sweet potatoes and regular ones. The girdle [griddle] from my granny is a family heirloom and virtually indestructible.' The scones are also good with houmous or tapenade, 'for that fusion experience unheard of in my granny's Lochaber!'

Tattie Scones

makes 8

Sue says: This is my own scone recipe especially for Bill.

1 large potato (about 250g/9 oz)
25g/1 oz unsalted butter, plus
    extra for frying and serving

50g/2 oz plain flour
½ tsp salt
¼ tsp baking powder

Peel the potato, cut into chunks and cook in a pan of boiling water until tender, then drain well. Using a potato masher, mash the potato with the butter. Now weigh it: you need about 200g/7 oz mash.

Sift the flour, salt and baking powder into a bowl. While the mash is still warm, stir into the flour and combine well. Using lightly floured hands, gently shape this mixture into 2 balls and turn out onto a lightly floured surface. With a rolling pin, roll out gently to form 2 circles about 5mm/¼ in thick. Cut each circle into quarters. Prick all over with a fork.

Heat the girdle, or griddle (or heavy frying pan) to medium-hot, smear over a little butter then, once hot, transfer 4 scones to it with a large spatula or fish slice. Cook for about 3–4 minutes each side until golden brown. Transfer to a wire rack to cool briefly before spreading with a little butter and eating warm.

They can also be made in advance; loosely wrap them in foil and reheat them in a low oven when needed.

Viv Lumsden, broadcaster
born 1952

Viv Lumsden's first memories of food involve soup. 'There was always a pot of soup on the go – some dead beasties' bones would be boiling away in the kitchen every single day. It was mainly Scotch broth, and that is the one soup I never make now as I never liked the barley in it.'

Growing up in Edinburgh, Viv enjoyed good food at home. Although her mother was a 'modern working mother', and so more into quick food such as mince and tatties and beans on toast, her grandmother was a very good home cook. 'I called my grandmother (my mum's mum) Dan – and she was an angel, looked just like Maw Broon, very stout with a little bun on her head! She did great soups.'

Viv also used to love her grandmother's meatloaf, made with minced steak, minced ham and sausagemeat (bound with breadcrumbs and an egg). But this versatile mixture was also used as a casing for her grandmother's Scotch eggs, which she used to enjoy. Sometimes her grandmother would cook a whole ox tongue: 'It used to boil away for hours, all curled up in an enormous pan.' Another childhood favourite, albeit a rather unhealthy one, was salad cream sandwiches; beans on toast was also an almost daily staple.

Since her own family were not pudding people, Viv remembers really well her grandmother's cheese soufflé and her steamed puds, 'with the greaseproof paper and string tied intricately round the top then made into a handle. There was syrup and raisin, cloutie dumpling or apple sponge – there was always some spongey thing going on.' And Viv mentions that, although they would have three courses at least once a day, portions were so much smaller than now and, although it was perhaps not as varied as these days, their diet was balanced – and always reflected what was in season.

Viv's family never ate out when she was a child, but if they were on holiday and ate in the restaurant of the hotel, her father, 'whose taste was very narrow', would opt for a plain omelette (cheese omelette if he was feeling daring), or steak on special occasions. She recalls on rare trips going to Jenners for afternoon tea: one of her mother's friends was a model who used to go round the tables posing during tea, displaying the store's clothes to the ladies as they supped from their porcelain cups.

Viv has always loved potatoes: 'It's my home vegetable. I love potatoes of all description and never enjoyed plain boiled rice. One other thing I disliked as a child – apart from barley – was fish with bones. My mum would go to Musselburgh especially to buy her smokies or kippers, and as she arrived home drooling in anticipation of the fish, I was dreading the bones.'

Viv seems to find herself returning more and more now to the old Scots dishes such as mince, skirlie and soups. Another soup she remembered her other grandmother making was butter bean and Savoy cabbage, which she loathed as butter beans were – and still are – one of her top most hated foods. Turnip remains one of her favourite vegetables, though, and she remembers fondly the particular smell of the burnt lid on the turnip lantern that all Scottish children used to take round when guysing at Hallowe'en, having spent hours howking out the impenetrable insides of the neep. Happy days...

Cheese Soufflé
serves 2–3

Not really a soufflé, more of a baked cheese pudding, but a great favourite; this is one of my grandmother's recipes.

300ml/10 fl oz/1½ cups milk
55g/2 oz/1 cup fresh breadcrumbs
15g/½ oz butter
1 large egg, beaten

55g/2 oz grated cheese
½ tsp mustard (dried)
salt and pepper, to taste

Heat the milk until it reaches boiling point, then remove from the heat and add the breadcrumbs and butter.

Mix well with a fork or wooden spoon. Add the remaining ingredients, pour into an oven dish and bake in an oven preheated to 180°C/350°F/Gas 4 for about half an hour until just set.

Alex McLeish, footballer
born 1959

Alex's first memories of eating involve Farley's rusks; and these are very fond memories as he adored them well into his teens when, instead of having them soaked in hot milk, he would dunk them into his tea.

But what he also recalls from his childhood is the weekly routine of meals, which meant that Tuesday was always Mince Day. He was never a lover of mince; he used to hate the fatty bits and would pick out any greasy blobs. Now he adores steak mince without fat. Another night was The Fry Up, which would involve bacon, egg, tattie scone and, of course, a 'butcher's slice' – also known as square sausage or Lorne sausage, a square beef sausage. Another routine was Saturday morning, football day, when he would go to collect the papers and pick up the morning rolls: well-fired Glasgow rolls. These would be eaten with either bacon or a 'square slice'. Alex still enjoys these: 'When you develop a taste for these foods as a child, it never changes; I love them!'

Although he sometimes had to have school dinners during his Glasgow childhood (he lived in the East End, then Kinning Park, then moved to Barrhead when he was five), he also liked coming home at lunchtime. One of the things he would love for a home lunch was Smash (packet mashed potatoes) mixed with grated cheese. When I asked him about it, he told me, 'It's got to be packet. And though my tastes have – thankfully – evolved since, I still love it as a treat!'

Another childhood treat was toasted cheese at night; and egg in a cup, especially when he was ill in bed. This was an 'almost hard-boiled' egg (he did not like them runny), mashed with butter and salt and eaten in a cup with a spoon. His wife sometimes makes that for him these days, though he proudly says that is one of the few things he actually cooks himself at home.

The family never ate out, but on Friday night, when his dad got his wages slip, they would sometimes have fish and chips from the chip shop. When he was about thirteen or fourteen, he began to make good progress in both his school football team and the local football club, and his dad started insisting on buying him a chicken breast for tea on a Friday night to 'build him up' for Saturday's game. And so began the demise of the greasy Friday-night fish supper!

There was little he did not like to eat as a child. If he had a couple of shillings spare, he loved to buy a big cream meringue or a fresh cream strawberry tart from the baker's. His all-time favourite was a Paris bun with crunchy sugar on top. He also loved stovies, usually served just as it came, but when he moved to Aberdeen in 1976 he often had it with corned beef.

'Although my mother made fantastic soups, I hated lentil soup; I really didn't like the texture. But her greatest dish was steak and kidney pie, baked in an ashet [enamel pie dish] and served with beef link sausages. My granny made steak pie, too, and I have an early memory of sitting on my grandad's lap as he was eating straight from the ashet. I remember him feeding me bits of pastry and gravy from the wonderful pie made by Granny.'

Steak pie was the New Year's Day meal, always served with link sausages and often with kidneys in it too. This was usually served with boiled potatoes, but young Alex liked to re-invent his Smash dish by removing the skins from the boiled potatoes and mashing the insides down with lots of butter.

One of Alex's favourite dishes was macaroni cheese, which was a family regular. When I asked what it was served with, he said 'Well, certainly never with salad. It was served just by itself!'

Macaroni Cheese
serves 4

Sue says: Although Alex would disapprove, my dish is delicious served with roasted cherry tomatoes or a simple tomato salad and some crusty bread.

250g packet of Marshalls' macaroni
45g/1½ oz butter
50g/1¾ oz flour
500ml/16 fl oz whole milk

175g/6 oz grated Cheddar
salt and pepper, to taste
a handful each of fresh breadcrumbs
and grated Cheddar, for topping

Boil the macaroni according to the packet instructions, then drain.

Meanwhile, melt the butter in a large saucepan, add the flour and, stirring well, cook for 2–3 minutes. Gradually whisk in the milk and simmer gently, whisking, for 10 minutes, then add the cheese and season to taste.

Stir the macaroni into the sauce, then tip it all into a shallow baking dish. Top with the breadcrumbs and extra cheese. Bake in an oven preheated to 180°C/350°F/Gas 4 for about 30 minutes.

Sir David Steel, politician, 1st Presiding Officer of the Scottish Parliament
born 1938

Sir David Steel was born in Kirkcaldy but brought up in both Kenya and Scotland, so his childhood memories also include less typically Scottish dishes such as home-made ice cream and fools made from tropical fruit.

His earliest memory, however, is even more unusual: 'I remember having to eat the rabbits kept in an outhouse during wartime rationing; this, however, was better than having to wear the smelly mittens made from their inadequately cured skins!'

One dish from his childhood that David still craves is good old mince and tatties; indeed, he asks, 'Why on earth can one never get that in restaurants in Scotland?'

A dish he loathed as a child growing up during the war was toad-in-the-hole, as it was made from wartime sausages and powdered egg. But he fondly recalls his mother's glorious dish of tripe and onions served with mashed potatoes – which she refused to eat herself!

One of David's favourite Scottish dishes nowadays is a good haggis with bashed neeps and champit tatties, but the one that reminds him most of his childhood is Welsh rarebit, which I have renamed Scottish rarebit for this book.

Scottish Rarebit

serves 1

Sue says: **Here is my own rarebit recipe for David.**

75g/2¾ oz Scottish farmhouse
   Cheddar, grated
1 tsp flour
2 tbsp milk
2 thick slices of bread
   (preferably wholemeal)

1 tsp Dijon mustard
1 tsp Worcestershire sauce
cayenne pepper, to taste

Put the cheese in a saucepan with the flour and milk and heat gently, stirring well, and put the bread on to toast. Once the cheese has melted, add the mustard and Worcestershire sauce. As soon as the mixture is smooth, pour it over the toast and shake over some pepper. Pop under a hot grill until golden.

Kirsty Wark, broadcaster
born 1955

Because her mother's family were the first commercial tomato growers on the Clyde, Kirsty Wark recalls halcyon days as a little girl, being surrounded by tomato plants. She vividly remembers being with her mother and aunt during the one day a year that was devoted to bottling. She came to understand the concept of 'home-made' very early on.

She also came to appreciate food in a rather un-Scottish way: by actually talking about its taste and feel and smell! As a child she was aware of the texture and aroma of the tomatoes, as she would be invited to touch and smell them. She also fondly remembers the fabulous taste of freshly made strawberry jam on white bread with butter.

Her mother always had a pot of soup on the go, and so too now does Kirsty. She sees cooking as very much a family thing – her son and husband cook, her daughter bakes and Kirsty does both. Even now she will make beef tea if someone is unwell, as that was the invalid food served when she was growing up: beef tied tightly in a pot with wax paper and string and boiled, then strained before being supped in bed.

But as for day-to-day meals, Kirsty reveals, 'there was always a routine when I was a child: a roast on Sundays, perhaps cauliflower cheese one night, then liver or haddock (smoked or fresh) on other nights of the week. And as a treat, a Green's crème caramel!' But there was very little that was not home-made, and Kirsty's mother's cake tins were always full. Favourites included tea bread (the loaf mixture soaked in tea overnight) and shortbread (her mother's was the best, with just a touch of cornflour to add a melt-in-the-mouth texture).

Kirsty enjoyed cooking as a child, and as well as the usual Scottish fare, she also remembers such exotic ingredients as melons being in the kitchen. These were such a treat: her mother would remove the seeds and place them in the oven to dry, then make necklaces with them! She also recalls dipping rhubarb into white sugar at her paternal grandmother's house, but since Kirsty lived in Kilmarnock, the first area in Scotland to have fluoride in the water, her teeth are not quite as full of fillings as most other 1950s rhubarb-dipping Scots children!

Kirsty seldom follows a recipe, but when she looks at her mother's old ones, perhaps smattered with butter, she says, 'I see these old recipes as a very tangible way of connecting with the past.'

Tomato Sauce
serves 4

I like serving this delicious sauce with pasta.

900g/2 lb halved and seeded tomatoes
 (skin on)
sea salt and black pepper, to sprinkle
olive oil, for drizzling and cooking
1 tsp sugar

3 cloves garlic, peeled and finely
 chopped
2 leeks, white part finely chopped
1 red onion, peeled and finely chopped

Liberally sprinkle the tomatoes with sea salt and black pepper and drizzle with olive oil. Roast in an oven preheated to 180°C/350°F/Gas 4 for 30 minutes.

Heat a little more olive oil with the sugar and sauté the garlic, leeks and onion until softened. Purée together with the tomatoes and serve with any type of cooked pasta.

Midge Ure, musician
born 1953

Midge Ure's earliest memory of food was mince, potatoes and butter beans – 'classic Scottish fare'. He remembers food being important, as he grew up in a tenement in Glasgow in the 1950s. Midge's dad was a van driver for a bakery, so he used to come home with tea cakes, morning rolls and crusty loaves, and his dad's father was a butcher, so he remembers having good sausages and stewing steak whenever his grandfather visited.

'We were never really into puddings. Besides, as there wasn't a table in the house until I was ten, we just ate on our laps so there was little time for two courses. We then moved out of the tenement into a modern council house with a bit more space for a table. But I do remember Creamola custard and some steamed puddings, especially a Heinz steamed syrup pudding in a tin that you had to pierce before boiling in a pan.

'One of my favourite dishes was stovies, but then I love peasant food throughout the world, whether it's pulses, potatoes or noodles. Stovies is our equivalent, a dish simply made of potatoes, onions and dripping. My granny made another of my favourites, which she called "Hot Chow". It was a stew made from potatoes, sausages and baked beans and was a derivation of stovies; quite weird, but delicious!'

Midge enjoyed fish suppers as a child and remembers that in Scottish chip shops all that was on offer was haddock, either battered or breadcrumbed. When he was older he used to try such treats as deep-fried black pudding or sausages, too.

There was only one thing he loathed as a child and that was offal. 'My dad used to eat lots of offal, such as liver and kidneys; he also ate tripe which I thought was so horrible as it looked just like a baby's nappy! If I even see a steak pie that has kidneys in it, I can't go near it.'

When Midge returns to Scotland he loves to go back to the places of his childhood and eat things he enjoyed then, such as a good Scotch pie from the butcher's or Lorne sausage with a fried egg and fried potato scone.

New Year was the only time that Midge's family ate anything that was traditional: 'We ate dinner at 10pm on Hogmanay; it was always an unusually late meal and it was always steak pie, which Mum used to make.' The pie was served with mashed potatoes and peas.

Nowadays he doesn't cook much in the way of Scottish dishes, as his one attempt at recreating the wonderful cloutie dumpling that was always made on birthdays was not entirely successful. 'I was so ham-fisted with it. But a dumpling to me is classic *Oor Wullie* stuff, with the ceremony of unwrapping the cloth and all.'

One of the dishes he does cook a lot these days is Blue Cheese Pasta, using a recipe given to him by his friend Mick Karm, bassist from the band Japan, who taught Midge to cook this simple but delicious dish.

Blue Cheese Pasta
serves 3–4

150g/5½ oz Stilton, crumbled
1 small tub Greek yoghurt
50g/1¾ oz pine nuts

300g/10 oz penne pasta
freshly ground black pepper, to taste

Melt the cheese very, very slowly in a pan until molten (do not overheat). Allow to cool until warm then slowly stir in the yoghurt until creamy.

Meanwhile, lightly toast the pine nuts in a hot pan until golden and tip into the sauce.

Cook the pasta according to the packet instructions then drain and tip into the sauce, tossing together with plenty of freshly ground black pepper. Serve warm.

Alan Cumming, actor
born 1965

Alan Cumming's earliest food memory is 'having mashed tattie sandwiches whilst pedalling round the kitchen in Fassfearn, near Fort William. They are an overlooked delicacy, I think!'

Food was very important in Alan's home because they lived in the country and couldn't just pop out to get something. His mum cooked and baked constantly, and indeed still does. Alan used to love her apple pies 'because the pastry had patterns of leaves on it'.

Even now he still craves stovies, which he finds so comforting and often makes in his own home: 'And they also remind me of parties and happy times. I actually really love dishes that are just one thing, instead of lots of different bits to choose from.'

On occasional trips to the chip shop as a child, his preference was always for white pudding suppers over fish suppers – and it still is. 'White pudding rules!' he says.

Touching on dishes he did not like, though, Alan told me: 'I hated celery. My mum used to make celery soup and it made me gag. Nowadays, though, I like celery. But I did learn a lot from watching my mum. I love making soup and hearty things like that, but I pretty much will have a bash at anything, especially in my house in upstate New York, because, like my childhood, it's the kind of place that you have to cook at home because you are up a mountain and there is no other alternative.'

When he returns to Scotland, Alan loves eating white pudding suppers – 'and the seafood always tastes so much better in Scotland. I am getting good at making my own cullen skink too.'

The mention of New Year brings back many happy memories for Alan: 'I used to love the spread that my parents would put out on Hogmanay, a real mix of sandwiches and cake and scones and nuts and all sorts. I do love a smorgasbord!'

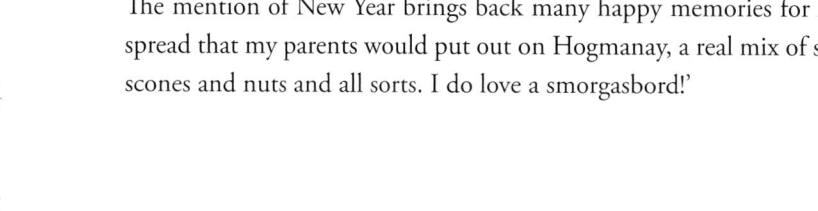

Vegetarian Stovies
serves many

Stovies is a Scottish dish that is traditionally made with beef dripping, but I am a vegetarian so I have made up my own version. It is real peasant food and ideal for people who, like me, like to have a plateful of one thing. I much prefer a mush-style dish to something with loads of different components.

Stovies are so great for parties on cold winter nights because you can just leave them on the stove and people can help themselves throughout the night as they please.

olive oil
3–4 cloves of garlic (more, if you like)
4 large onions
8–10 large potatoes

tamari or dark soy sauce, to taste
Worcestershire sauce, to taste
salt and pepper, to taste
a couple of handfuls of soya mince

In a wok or large pot, put a good old sloosh of olive oil. (I normally turn the bottle upside down and count until about four.) Chop up some garlic, and fry it in the olive oil for a bit. Don't let them get crispy, but they need to permeate the oil and make a tasty base for the stovies.

Take the biggish onions and chop them up (fairly big chunks, not that sort of manic onion slush that fancy chefs do) and add them to the olive oil and garlic. Fry them for a bit longer then put a lid on and leave them to sweat for a bit (about 5 minutes).

Now scrub and chop up the potatoes. Chop them into fairly big, mouthful-size chunks. Add the potatoes to the sweating onions and garlic and leave them for a bit to get all infused.

Now comes the fun bit. Get your tamari or dark soy sauce and squirt about 20 or so squirts into the wok, then do the same with your Worcestershire sauce. You could also use BBQ sauce or something like that; basically the trick is to make the stovies tasty and to give it a bit of a browny colour. You do all this to taste, and you can also add some salt and pepper if you like (although don't go crazy with the salt if you are going heavy on the tamari).

Then throw in a couple of big handfuls of the TVP, aka Textured Vegetable Protein (I like to call it soya mince because TVP sounds strange. Rather funnily my assistant, Joey, thought I said soya mints the first time I asked him to buy some and he had a devil of a job tracking any down). The thing with the soya mince is that it swells up in the water and gives the stovies some nice texture and taste and also makes it thicker. So if your stovies are too runny, throw in some more to them thicken up. *Continued overleaf.*

Vegetarian Stovies

continued

Pour water into the wok so that all the ingredients are just submerged. Bring to the boil for a bit, turn it down to simmer, then go away and check your email or have a bath or something. Stir occasionally, and once the potatoes are cooked you can give them a little beating up with a spoon to make the stovies more mushy.

I usually cook mine for about 30 minutes, with the lid half on, half off. Then you can turn them off, put the lid on and let them cook in their own juices.

As you will have noticed, I don't really do precise measurements when I cook. Basically this is a mushy, potato stewy thing that can come in various consistencies and you just have to find the combination that suits you best. You could also add things like hot sauce or mustard if you felt daring. Enjoy!

Sue says: This dish requires no additional salt if you are using both tamari sauce and Worcestershire sauce.

fish

Lorraine Kelly, broadcaster
born 1959

When asked, Lorraine easily remembered her earliest food memory: 'That would be my Granny Kelly making me egg in a cup, and also my mum's home-made Scotch broth, which I have tried to copy and even though I follow her recipe to the letter, it is never as good.'

Food was very important in the Kelly house: Lorraine's maternal grandmother, Margaret McMahon, was a chef and her mum is a really good cook – nothing fancy, just well-cooked proper food like mince and potatoes, roast dinners, grilled fish, and so on.

'I loved Heinz tomato soup', Lorraine says, 'with a spoonful of my mum's light and fluffy creamy mashed potato plonked in the middle; also haddock poached in milk and boiled ham and cabbage. My Granny Kelly used to make wonderful dumplings that she put in a pillow case and boiled.'

According to Lorraine, you didn't really eat out much in those days but her parents were adventurous eaters. 'When I was about twelve they discovered Shenaz – which must have been one of the first, if not *the* first Indian restaurant in Glasgow – opposite the Mitchell Library. I would have *pakora*, which Latif the owner called "indescribables" and chicken biryani and chapati bread. Dad would have beef special curry, *tinda* (Indian gourd) and naan. It was wonderful food.' The family would also go to Italian restaurants in Glasgow for pasta and ice cream.

Fish suppers were another real treat, but her mum cooked a lot of fish at home – lemon sole being Lorraine's favourite. Her mum always spent money on really good food for Lorraine and her brother Graham.

However, one thing that Lorraine loathed was mashed potatoes mixed with cheese: 'It always made me feel ill, but I ate most things even though I wasn't that keen on green vegetables.' But at New Year she did eat cabbage; on that day it just had to be steak pie from the butcher's with potatoes, neeps, cabbage and tons of black pepper.

These days her husband Steve does most of the cooking, and they have a lot of Scottish food such as scallops, fish, beef and venison. 'Good Scottish cooking', she says proudly, 'is terrific, and when you get top-class ingredients, you can't beat it.'

Scallops with Black Pudding and Buster Peas

serves 3–4

Sue says: Buster peas are Dundee's answer to mushy peas, although to me and to fellow Dundonians like Lorraine's husband, Steve, they are better. Traditionally they were simply marrowfat peas cooked until soft, flavoured with plenty of salt, pepper and vinegar, then served with chips. My version for Lorraine is not exactly what Dundee might recognise, but it is delicious!

300g/10 oz peas (fresh or frozen)
400g tin of butter beans, drained
juice of 1 large lemon
1 garlic clove, peeled
extra virgin olive oil

salt and pepper, to taste
3–4 slices of black pudding (preferably Stornoway black pudding)
9–12 scallops

For the peas, cook them in a pan of boiling water until just done, then drain and run under a cold tap to arrest cooking and retain their bright green colour. Thoroughly pat dry on kitchen paper then tip into a food processor with the beans, lemon juice and garlic. Whiz briefly then add enough olive oil – about 5 tablespoons – to form a thickish purée, seasoning to taste. Set aside.

Heat 2 tablespoons of the oil in a frying pan then, once hot, add the black pudding slices and fry until crispy – a couple of minutes each side. Remove to a warm plate lined with kitchen paper. Increase the heat under the pan, add the scallops and fry for 1–2 minutes on each side, depending on their thickness.

To serve, place a dollop of the warm buster peas on warm plates and top with a slice of black pudding then the scallops.

George Robertson,
Lord Robertson of Port Ellen,
Secretary General of NATO 1999–2004
born 1946

George Robertson's first memory of food in his early childhood on the island of Islay was of porridge: porridge with syrup served up in the police station. George's father was a policeman, and indeed most of his family – grandparents, brother, son – have ended up as policemen. George is the exception.

There was always freshly cooked food at home both in Islay and when the family moved to Dunoon when he was six. George remembers tripe, pigs' trotters and one of his great favourites – mince and potatoes, although since he has 'an acute aversion' to onions, mince often caused problems. It's the same with leeks and any of the onion family; and garlic makes him ill, too. But, fortunately, there was little call for garlic in the west of Scotland in the 1950s.

George also loved chicken noodle soup; other soups and broths he always had to have strained in case a stray onion was lurking. He remembers excellent local meat on Islay, and although shellfish is now very popular, it was never eaten locally; indeed, George told me 'the fishermen used to throw the prawns back into the sea. But our family sometimes bought prawns from the local fishermen so we could enjoy them at home.' He also loved Lorne (square) sausage, potted hough and steak pie. And for pudding, there was bread and butter pudding, tapioca, steamed pudding, cloutie dumpling – and home baking. 'I especially remember the pancakes being made on the girdle [griddle], then eating them with butter and jam.'

'School dinners were not only horrible [lumpy custard, watery mince – this latter with, of course, the inherent onion problem], but there was also a social problem as, since we normally went home for lunch, we were frozen out by the regular school-dinner children!'

George never learned to cook or bake at home, and even at university, when most of us were attempting spaghetti Bolognese, he only ever cooked potatoes. He and I both recalled Greasy Pete's, the famous chip shop on Dundee's Hawkhill, near his university flat. He also told me about a time he was invited to a fellow student's house for a meal. He was very fond of this girl but was apprehensive when he didn't know what she was cooking. When it turned out to be risotto he thought he would try it, but after one mouthful of a dish that contained more onions than he had eaten in all his life – that was that: an end not only to the evening, but to a beautiful friendship!

Although the family never ate out when he was young, George remembers either going on occasion to a hotel or to relatives for high tea. On his father's side there were farmers and George remembered fondly the freshly cooked dishes – local mutton or lamb and vegetables. 'When we had a meal there, we used to eat everything on the same plate: we had soup in a deep plate first, then, once that was finished, the meat and vegetables would be served in it too.'

Although this scallop dish does not exactly sum up his childhood diet, it is something he enjoys and which shows off the prime ingredients from his childhood home, Islay, to perfection. But remember: no onions!

Islay Scallop Salad with Asparagus

serves 3–4

Sue says: My recipe hopefully meets with George's approval.

olive oil, for cooking
12 plump scallops
1 large bag of interesting salad leaves,
    washed

200g/7 oz fine asparagus,
    lightly cooked

For the vinaigrette:
1 tbsp sherry vinegar
½ tsp Dijon mustard
sea salt and freshly ground black
    pepper, to taste

approx. 4 tbsp extra virgin
    olive oil

First, make the vinaigrette. Mix the vinegar and mustard and some sea salt in a small bowl. Using a small whisk, whisk in the oil to make an emulsion. Check the seasoning, adding some black pepper.

Pour 1 tablespoon of oil into a heavy frying pan and heat until very hot. Once it is searing hot (this will take a couple of minutes) add half the scallops (they will spit) and cook for 2–3 minutes, turning after 1 minute, then remove and keep warm. Cook the remaining scallops in more oil, if necessary.

Meanwhile, toss the salad leaves in a bowl with the vinaigrette, then top with the seared scallops and asparagus. Serve with crusty bread.

Sheena Macdonald, broadcaster
born 1954

Sheena Macdonald was familiar with the concept of bribery from an early age. Her earliest food memory was 'when I was aged about two or three, sitting on the manse kitchen table, bawling. My mother wanted to cut my toenails and said to me I could have some of her syllabub if I allowed her to get out the scissors. Even though I remember realising I would lose out as I had to endure the toenail cutting, clearly the bribery worked!'

Since Sheena's mother is an excellent cook and baker, the reward made it worthwhile. There were many tins full of her mum's excellent cakes and pies; she recalls her mum's wonderful shortbread and pastry being rolled out and the little pastry cutters on the kitchen table; and vividly remembers the joy of licking the bowl after a cake had been made.

Now Sheena thinks most fondly of classics such as mince and potatoes, and has less of the Scots sweet tooth, but when the family moved from the Limekilns Church in Fife, where her father was a Church of Scotland minister, to Mayfair Church in Edinburgh, they were not far from the McVitie's biscuit factory on Causewayside. 'This is where my mum would buy tins of broken biscuits, which I adored, but only when eaten in sequence: at high tea at 6pm, after the savoury course, plain bread and butter had to be eaten first, then bread, butter and jam, then those adored plain digestive biscuits and then (especially if my grandmother had brought Penguins) chocolate biscuits.'

There was also a ritual to Friday night, when she would go to Brownies bearing sixpence: threepence for subs, the other threepence for chips on the way home, doused with salt and vinegar (never brown sauce). And although it might have seemed ahead of its time, another popular modern Scottish takeaway was a regular at the Macdonald manse: since her father had served in the Indian army, curry was a great favourite. Sheena's mum also made it herself very well and very hot, and though it was served with boiled rice, Sheena loathed rice pudding and still does.

But she recalls another milk pudding with more nostalgia: school dinner semolina with jam, which you swirled round to make it bright pink. The school custard was, however, vile; all lumpy or with a thick skin on top. (I, too, can remember this, since Sheena and I were at the same school. I reminded her about the thick globby custard in the white jugs at the school dinner tables often changing colour – bright white to go with chocolate sponge or lurid pink to go with plain sponge: both equally repellent.)

Although she never had them as a child, Sheena loves Scottish mussels and adores cooking them these days. Perhaps some of the wine left over from the mussel dish can be used to whip up a syllabub for pudding, although Sheena is unsure whether the use of alcohol would have been permitted in the manse syllabub!

Mussels in Wine
serves 3–4

Sue says: Sheena's husband, Allan Little, likes cream on his mussels (although Sheena does not), so I have added it as an option with a pinch of saffron threads towards the end of my recipe, for those who also like creamy mussels. Serve with plenty of slices of baguette.

50g/1¾ oz butter
1 large leek finely sliced (or 1 onion, peeled and chopped)
2 garlic cloves, peeled and chopped
150ml/5 fl oz white wine
1kg/2 lb 4 oz mussels, scrubbed, debearded

150ml/5 fl oz double cream (optional)
pinch of saffron threads (optional)
salt and pepper, to taste
3 tbsp flat-leaved parsley, chopped

Heat the butter in a large saucepan and gently fry the leek (or onion) and garlic until softened, then increase the heat and add the wine. Bring to the boil then immediately add the mussels, put on a tight lid and cook over a high heat for 2–3 minutes or until they are just beginning to open.

If using cream, add this now with the saffron and continue to heat for another couple of minutes, until the mussels are fully open. (If not adding cream, continue cooking until the shells open.)

Remove from the heat, season with salt and pepper to taste, then stir in the parsley and serve in warm bowls (discarding any unopened mussels).

Mary Contini, author and Director of Valvona & Crolla
born 1956

Mary Contini remembers much about her childhood, spent with her seven siblings in a house above the Cockenzie Café where her father Johnny Di Ciacca sold fish and chips and ice cream. Her first food memory is of the smell of sweet, warm milky custard permeating the whole house. Once the 'mix' was boiled, it ran through stainless steel pipes then appeared on top of the cooler where it flowed down corrugated steel 'like a milk waterfall' before being collected in steel pails, chilled, then churned. 'I still remember the intensity of that sweet vanilla smell,' says Mary, 'and the noise of it being delivered in gallon containers at about 6am'. Another flashback was to their kitchen dining table when her older brother and sister (Mary was third of the eight children) had gone back to school but come home for lunch. Mary remembers eating nibbles of the food her siblings had left, so she must have had a healthy appetite! There was plenty of good food for the family, but it was very much run according to old-fashioned standards: the older children, and the boys in particular, always got the better cuts and better food, which was always home-cooked.

Food was hugely important in the Di Ciacca home: at the back of the house there was a hut on the shore which was used for the chip shop. It smelled very much of jute sacks as this is where the potatoes were sorted to be peeled and cut into chips. On the other side of the hut was a derelict building where her dad cleaned the fish, wearing rubber wellies and a long rubber apron (as opposed to his role in the ice-cream shop where he wore white wellies and a white coat). He would gut and fillet 8–10 boxes of fish, usually haddock, which were cooked in dripping. A lady called Margaret who helped Mary's mum with the ironing and also worked in both the shops, used to make the children fritters: thick slices of potatoes dipped in batter and deep-fried – a real luxury.

When Mary was growing up there was both Italian and Scottish food: since her mum also ran the café in Port Seton, they would all be fed what was on the menu there – boiled ham, steak pie – but on a Sunday there was only Italian food. As a treat, her parents would go to the famous Italian deli Valvona & Crolla to indulge, so the Sunday meal would start with '*sugo* and socks' (home-made tomato *sugo* or sauce with rigatoni), then either *spalebone* or minceballs cooked in the *sugo*, then, of course, ice cream with strawberries or raspberries, if the season was right.

Instead of having Parmesan with their pasta the Di Ciaccas always had pecorino (ewe's milk cheese), as that was from the south of Italy where Mary's family was from. Indeed, sometimes a parcel would arrive at the house from the Italian mountain villages – very exciting. 'When I was about thirteen, the Italian family sent a large basket of fresh figs, which I had never tasted. My parents showed me how to peel them open then eat the delicious flesh.'

Margaret, the lady who helped the family, used to take at least five of the Di Ciacca kids to Peterhead, where she came from, for holidays. Mary used to love staying with her family (all fishermen), except for the food: the mince and tatties were just not to her liking, as she was only used to being fed by her mum. Similarly, when she had to have school dinners she hated them, and Mary remembers smuggling in bottles of HP sauce to try to make the food on her plate more palatable.

Mary was taught to cook not only by her mother but also by both her *nonnas* (grandmothers) and also, once she had married Philip, by her mother-in-law, Olivia Contini, who would teach her to cook her new husband's favourite dishes, such as cabbage soup with fonteluna sausage.

'As well as eating a lot of fish and chips every Friday, being a good Catholic family, we would have *pasta e patate* (pasta and potato soup) followed by fried fish – often lemon sole, if that was available. And with the extended family we would sometimes go on picnics down the coast, but instead of the usual Scottish sandwiches and chocolate biscuits, we would take huge frittata and *pastone* – ham and egg pie. We would also set up pans and stoves on the beach and cook pasta with *sugo* for the throngs.'

Because of the Port Seton café, a lot of home baking was needed. Mary remembers her mum making huge trays of shortbread (180 pieces in one tray!), scones, fairy cakes and 'apple pies to die for'. She also remembers the downside of her mum doing outside catering – for the miners' clubs and fishermen's dances – such as having to peel potatoes for 250 people, sometimes three times a week. The Di Ciaccas often had family Christmas in the café, as there was more room there. 'From the time I was ten I can remember we'd feed the five thousand there – well, forty to forty-five people probably – *sugo* and home-made pasta with meatballs, then turkey or roast beef, then, of course, our own ice cream and Yum Yum pudding, which is a lighter Christmas pudding.'

Mary is passionate about Scottish food, having been brought up on good, honest local ingredients: 'In my experience of food all over, our Scottish ingredients are so superior; we Scots really ought to just stop and take a look at what is around us.'

Fish Supper
serves 2

You can't re-create the flavour and texture of fish fried in fifty litres of melted lard at home: don't try it! But you can shallow-fry fresh haddock, coated in egg and breadcrumbs, and make a delicious supper easily.

2 fresh haddock fillets bought from
    a good fishmonger (or fillets of cod,
    lemon sole or witch sole)
4–5 tbsp plain flour

2 eggs, beaten and seasoned
4–5 tbsp fresh breadcrumbs
corn oil or sunflower oil, for frying

For the chips:
4 floury potatoes, such as Maris Piper
    or King Edward

corn oil or sunflower oil, for frying

To make the fish: wash it first. (Most people are put off fish because of the taste of stale water that clings to its surface. It seems obvious, but always wash fish and shellfish in cold water and pat it dry before cooking.) Place the flour, eggs and breadcrumbs in 3 separate, shallow soup bowls.

Dip the haddock on both sides firstly in the flour then, shaking off any excess, dip it into the beaten egg, coating each side. Lastly, coat the haddock in the breadcrumbs, pressing it down to make sure the breadcrumbs stick.

Heat enough oil to coat the bottom of a large frying pan by at least 3cm/1½ in. Check that the oil is hot enough by dipping the end of the fillet into it. When it sizzles really well, it's ready. Lay the fish into the oil. Cook 1 or 2 fish at a time only; if you over-crowd the frying pan the oil will get too cold and the fish will be soggy instead of crisp. Keep the heat high so that the fish fry briskly.

Let the bottom of the fish crisp and brown before using a spatula and fork to carefully flip it over. When it is crisp on both sides, lift it with the spatula and drain the oil by putting it on kitchen paper.

To make the chips: peel the potatoes and cut them into chips, soaking them in cold water until ready to use. This stops the starch in the potatoes turning them black. Before cooking, rinse the chips to get rid of any starch and pat dry.

Heat the oil in a chip pan with a chip basket or in an electric fryer, if you have one. Test the temperature of the oil by putting one chip into it. As soon as it rises to the surface and starts to move around and sizzle, the oil is hot enough.

Add just enough chips so that they are well covered with oil. Too many chips and the temperature of the oil will fall and the chips will be soggy. Give the chip basket a good shake so that all the chips are free and coated with oil. Keep the heat at a brisk level so that the oil doesn't cool down, shaking the basket from time to time.

As the chips cook they will begin to colour. As they get darker and the sizzling slows down, they're ready. Lift the chips out of the oil and press one with your fingers to check that they're soft inside.

Drain them and put them into a bowl lined with kitchen paper. Whip the paper out and sprinkle them and the fish with sea salt. I love to eat this fish supper with fresh lemon juice squeezed all over it. Mmm...

There are some rules you need to know in order to deep-fry safely – here are Mary's: Use good, fresh oil: sunflower or corn oil is best. Use it once or twice only; after that the chemicals in the oil start to break down and the oil becomes fairly unhealthy.

Fill the fryer no more than half full. Once the food is added and starts to cook, the oil moves nearer the surface and can easily overflow.

Make sure the oil is hot before you start to fry. Add a chip or piece of bread to the oil, and when it comes to the surface, sizzles and moves around, the oil is hot enough.

Don't overcrowd the oil. Food needs space to move around, so cook fried foods in batches.

Make sure the food you are frying is dry; the combination of water and fat makes it splash dangerously.

Gavin Hastings, rugby player
born 1962

Gavin Hastings' earliest food memories when growing up in Edinburgh are of Sundays; all dressed up for Sunday school then going to his granny's for a Sunday lunch of mince and tatties, a great favourite of Gavin's. Then there would be a lovely pudding, such as apple or rhubarb crumble, before a family walk with his three brothers on the Braid Hills, with a ball. When I ask which shape, Gavin says, 'usually one of each – a round and an oval!'

Gavin remembers 'eating loads; I was always the big eater in the house and always asked for seconds'. His mum is a very good cook, having trained at the Edinburgh College of Domestic Science. He remembers every single day he and his brothers would have eggs – scrambled, poached, an omelette – and there was always a two-course, sometimes three-course, meal at night. His mum made wonderful home-made tomato soup (using a combination of fresh, tinned and puréed tomatoes) and lentil soup; her kedgeree was legendary, as was her meatroll and also her bacon and egg pies. Puddings might be a fruit crumble, a lemon meringue pie or the family favourite 'Oofum Floofum', also known in many other Scottish families as Jelly Fluff (chilled evaporated milk whipped up and mixed with melted jelly). The Hastings family version had Hundreds and Thousands on top, too!

Mrs Hastings also baked a lot for her continually ravenous sons. Gavin recalls coming home from school and devouring many rounds of toast and drinking milk straight from the bottle (which his mother disapproved of): 'We had six bottles of milk delivered by the milkman every day.' Then he would raid the cake tins, a particular favourite being a chocolate digestive biscuit traybake called tiffin. 'We usually demolished the entire batch at one go.'

Christmas was a special meal with the turkey and all the trimmings being preceded by his mum's famous tomato soup. As well as Christmas pudding with brandy butter, another favourite of Gavin's was the intriguingly named 'Uncle Tom's Pudding', which was a steamed treacle pudding made with black treacle and served with proper home-made custard.

When asked if there was anything he truly hated to eat as a child Gavin says, 'No, not really. I really did eat anything and everything and always asked for seconds.' But when I asked him about his cooking skills, he told me a story of a Sunday magazine that had wanted him to cook for a barbecue issue, so he agreed, thinking that he could at least do that. In between slamming bits of meat on the barbie for the photo shoot he was running around the garden after his then toddler son and so perhaps not giving the food his one-hundred per cent concentration. The headline of the article two weeks later therefore read 'During his career, Gavin Hastings faced many an All-Black, which is just about the same colour as the food coming off his barbecue!'

Gavin remembers playing football at Myreside in the early evening when it was dark and then having the treat of a fish supper on the way home, which he loved. But apart from that and the occasional Chinese restaurant dinner ('although with four boys we were always a rather noisy rabble eating out'), the everyday family meals were always taken with everyone sitting round the kitchen table, something he strongly believes in to this day with his own family.

Kedgeree
serves 6

approx. 680g/1 lb 8 oz long-grain rice
2–3 large fillets smoked haddock, cooked and flaked
6 hard-boiled eggs, peeled and quartered
75g/2¾ oz butter, for cooking

My mum cooked plenty of long-grain rice in a pan of boiling water until it was fluffy then mixed it with cooked, flaked smoked haddock and peeled and quartered hard-boiled eggs. She then melted lots of butter in a pan and gently combined everything – and that was that. Simple, but delicious!

Sue says: Although Gavin's mum's recipe is simply rice, fish, eggs and butter, I like to add some spring onions sautéed in butter, a little curry powder and some cherry plum tomatoes sliced in half.

Sir Menzies Campbell, MP and Leader of the Liberal Democrats 2006–2007
born 1941

Ming Campbell's earliest food memories while growing up in Glasgow are of his mother making huge pots of soup, using enormous ingenuity with few ingredients during the austerity of the Second World War and 1940s rationing. All the female members of his family were good cooks and excellent bakers, with his mum regularly rustling up scones, sponges and pancakes, although for special occasions she could also adeptly turn out the less everyday meringues and small fancy cakes. Having acquired a sweet tooth from birth (like most Scots), he has fond memories of puddings (still his favourite course), with syrup sponge even now much loved, as well as dishes such as trifle. 'Anything with custard always hit the spot – and still does,' he told me.

Ming hated vegetables such as cabbage, sprouts and carrots as a child, and now has a more sophisticated taste in vegetables, preferring asparagus and mangetout, both unheard of in Scotland during his childhood.

As a student living in a flat in Glasgow, he suddenly found he had to cook for himself and so mastered three simple dishes: steak, lamb chops and smoked haddock steamed in milk. He still loves a fish supper as an occasional indulgence: 'particularly in my constituency in the East Neuk of Fife, where the quality of fish is world class'.

When he returns to Scotland from Westminster, he enjoys variations on his student favourites – beef, lamb and fish – though he adds kippers to the list nowadays, as well as perhaps a little more sophistication all round. Although there is still always room for custard...

Smoked Haddock Pie

serves 4

The advantage of this dish is that it can be prepared in advance and can be kept warm for a good while in a low oven. It is one of my favourites.

butter, for greasing
225g/½ lb fresh spinach, lightly wilted
450g/1lb smoked haddock, cooked
   and flaked
6 hard-boiled eggs, sliced

6 tomatoes, sliced
salt and pepper, to taste
approx. 600ml/1pint cheese sauce,
   to cover

Butter an ovenproof dish and layer the ingredients in it, starting with the spinach, then the haddock, then the hard-boiled eggs, and finally the tomatoes. Season with salt and pepper between each layer. Finally, cover with the cheese sauce. Cook in an oven preheated to 180°C/350°F/Gas 4 for 30 minutes.

meat

Andy Murray, tennis player
born 1987

Andy Murray's first food memory is of tipping a plate of custard on his head when he was in his high chair! Apart from this trauma, he has good memories of food, as not only was his mum a good cook but 'My gran is an awesome cook. She studied at domestic science college. When I was wee I used to tell her she was "a great cooker".'

The favourite childhood dishes that Andy still craves are his gran's Greek shepherd's pie and his mum's fresh fruit salad. If the latter sounds more healthy than the choice of the average Scot, this is backed up by the fact Andy doesn't ever eat offerings from the chip shop – so no fish suppers, no white pudding suppers.

However, they did eat out occasionally when he was a child: 'There was an Italian café in Stirling called Corriers, where I always had pepperoni pizza and a coconut milkshake.'

Of all the food he was brought up with, the only thing he can remember truly despising was Christmas pudding, which he thought tasted just awful.

Andy learned the rudiments of cooking at home and some baking too: 'I remember making little sponge cakes and covering them with icing and Smarties. Nowadays I can make pretty good pasta with tomato sauce; and I make great smoothies; my top one is strawberry, raspberry and blueberry with a bit of yoghurt and honey – tremendous!'

 When he returns to Scotland now he likes to eat simple but good food: 'Steak with salad, fresh fruit salad and ice cream from the Bridge of Allan Café – or anything my gran makes me.'

Andy has very special memories of Christmas dinners at his gran's home: 'There was home-made turkey broth, roast turkey and all the trimmings, then fresh fruit salad and ice cream. The only problem was that my gran gave us the same sized portions from age five to eighteen, so Jamie and I were always starving. Eventually we had to tell her... and last year we got more than one chipolata each. Result!'

Greek Shepherd's Pie
serves 4

225g/½ lb onions
2 tbsp oil
450g/1 lb minced beef
1 tbsp chopped fresh parsley
175g/6 oz tomatoes

butter, for greasing
450g/1 lb potatoes, peeled and
   thinly sliced
salt and pepper, to taste

For the white sauce:
50g/1¾ oz butter
50g/1¾ oz flour

400ml/14 fl oz milk
2 tbsp grated cheese

Slice the onions thinly and fry gently in the oil in a large pan until soft, adding the mince and parsley after a few minutes and stirring from time to time. Slice the tomatoes, add to the meat and cook gently for 5 minutes.

Butter a round soufflé dish and arrange layers of overlapping potato slices on the bottom. Season with salt and pepper, then spread a layer of meat and tomatoes, then another layer of potatoes.

In a pan, make a thick sauce blending the butter and flour and then slowly adding the milk, stirring all the time. Season well and stir in the grated cheese. Pour over the potatoes and shake the dish so that the sauce penetrates.

Bake in an oven preheated to 180°C/350°F/Gas 4 for 1¼ hours or until the potatoes are tender. Serve with a green salad.

Nick Nairn, chef
born 1959

Nick Nairn remembers being about four years old and sat in the kitchen of their house in Boquhan, near Killearn (they had moved there from the family house at the Lake of Monteith for five years while his dad, Jimmy Nairn, was doing *The One O'Clock Gang Show* on television). He was watching his mum making soup and tried to copy her by doing it in a tin can. He chopped the vegetables – with a butter knife – stirred it with cold water in the can and wondered why on earth it was so repellent!

His mum was – and still is – a very good cook, and the family ate very well on a diet of salmon, game, beef and lamb. However, she always served plain fare because his dad reckoned that anything resembling 'foreign muck' – cooked with onions, garlic and herbs – was the 'work of the devil'. Nick was nineteen when he tasted his first curry – and that was in Asia. Both his grandmothers were good bakers, his dad's mum baking traditional things like scones and Black Bun; while his mum's mum made the very best scones – Nick can still remember the sight of a jug of milk souring on the windowsill, sour milk being the secret ingredient for the fabulous scones.

But it was his own mum's meatloaf, cooked in a glazed earthenware jar that he remembers as being his favourite, as well as tomato soup made with home-grown tomatoes, stock from a ham bone, onion, carrots and orange lentils. The meatloaf would be served with home-made chips and some of his dad's own tomatoes, cut thickly and dressed with nothing more than salt and pepper. 'The Nairns', said Nick, 'are obsessed with potatoes! Dad has always grown them and used to favour only the floury varieties, but now he is siding with me and enjoying more waxy varieties, such as Charlotte.'

They also grew fruit in the garden – rhubarb, raspberries and blackcurrants – and Nick's mum would make not only jam but blackcurrant jelly (which he recalls dripping through the multi-stained jeely bag suspended on a tripod). Nick admits, 'I tried to run away every time it was blackcurrant picking time as it was so mind-blowingly awful.' Nick's mum also makes the best pancakes ever, on her Aga, with 'the most sensational texture', but she is a perfectionist and will only serve up the perfect ones.

There was a shoot opposite their house on Lake of Monteith, so Nick's dad would often bring home pheasants which his mum would roast simply. He also smoked his own salmon – wild salmon brought from Helmsdale. For Nick, smoked salmon is still synonymous with Christmas Day, as when he was young they would have it with scrambled eggs for breakfast and then again as a simple starter at Christmas dinner.

Nowadays Nick cooks roast chicken at least once a week, making a risotto or pasta the second night and then using the wonderful stock either for soup or to add flavour to the other great family favourite, mince and tatties.

To appease his sweet tooth, Nick still adores custard with jam – 'Mum's was packet Bird's custard, served with some home-made strawberry jam. I still love that!' He also tells me about his dad's after-meal preference, which Nick obviously disapproves of: bread spread with butter and with white sugar sprinkled on top. 'A very Kirkintilloch post-war treat that he loves to this day,' says Nick.

'School dinners were repellent,' Nick told me, and having heard about one day's experience, this memory seems justified: Nick hated rice pudding anyway, but one he was served while at primary school was 'covered in skin and had lumps the size of golf balls in it'. The teacher forced him to eat it until he got halfway through, whereupon he vomited it all back into the bowl. You can imagine the rest: the bowl still had to be consumed... 'It's hardly surprising it took me twenty years to even touch rice pudding again!'

Meatloaf
serves 6

150g/5½ oz minced pork or bacon (use smoked bacon so you don't need to add salt)

450g/1 lb lean beef mince
2 tbsp fresh breadcrumbs, to bind

Mix all the ingredients together then pack them into a 900g/2 lb stone jar and seal it with a double layer of tin foil. Set the jar in boiling water in a tall casserole dish and simmer in an oven preheated to 180°C/350°F/Gas 4 for approximately 3 hours.

Serve with home-made chips and home-grown tomatoes.

Dougie Donnelly,
television sports presenter
born 1953

Dougie Donnelly remembers sitting in a high chair being spoon-fed from a tiny jar of baby food – it was puréed apples – and he loved it! A little later, when he was out of the high chair, the memory shifts to eating corned beef with baked beans; a great favourite, but he admits 'When I was very young, I did not exactly have a sophisticated palate!'

Food was important in the Donnelly household in Rutherglen as he grew up with two very good cooks: his mother and grandmother. 'My mother would make good, wholesome but traditional food such as meat, potatoes and two veg – but only after a plate of hearty soup. I ate everything and really had few favourites as it was all tasty. My mother's speciality soups were oxtail, which I loved, and also great, thick Scotch broths.'

His grandmother was the baker in the family and Dougie remembers helping her make Scotch pancakes, which he had to have all soft in the middle. Her speciality was little dark Coburg cakes. 'Another fond memory of baking days was, of course, licking the bowl!'

On Sundays there would be a roast dinner, usually beef (silverside a popular cut) or lamb, and for pudding, perhaps his mother's famous apple tart or apple sponge. 'Served with Crolla's fabulous Italian ice cream, this was heaven.'

The only thing he truly hated as a child was tripe and he remembers coming home from school and opening the door to the horrible smell of it cooking. He had to eat it but once he was older Dougie was eventually excused the torture.

The family seldom ate out but were allowed a treat of a fish supper if they had gone out for a drive. They collected fish and chips on the way home, though his dad hated the smell in the car!

Though he lives in Scotland, Dougie tends to be away travelling for some five months of the year, so loves to get home and to leave hotel food behind. These days, he gets stuck into fish and venison, cooked by his wife Linda who is great in the kitchen: 'We have such great Scottish produce, why look anywhere else for the best ingredients?'

Alligator Stew
serves 6

This is Linda's mum's recipe – basically a mince casserole – but a huge favourite in our family.

500g/1 lb 2 oz mince
pepper, to taste
1 large onion, peeled and sliced
4 medium potatoes, peeled and
    thinly sliced

840g tin of baked beans
400g tin of tomato soup
    (Heinz; or use Baxter's if you want
    to be posh!)

Brown the mince in a hot pan without extra fat, season well then tip into a casserole dish. Top with the onion then the potatoes. Spoon over the beans then finally pour over the soup. Bake in a preheated oven (180°C/450°F/Gas 4) for 1½ hours, until the potatoes are tender, then eat piping hot.

Sue says: I don't season the mince with salt, only pepper as there is enough salt in the 2 tins. I like to serve this with some good bread to dunk into the tomatoey juices – and a watercress salad.

Dame Evelyn Glennie,
virtuoso percussionist
born 1965

When I asked Evelyn Glennie if she thought her childhood, growing up on a farm in Aberdeenshire, was idyllic, she laughed and said, 'Now I think about it, it probably was! The family farm had beef cattle, dairy cows, sheep, hens and mixed arable. Everything was local: from eggs, milk and cheese off the farm to the vegetables and fruit from the garden.'

Evelyn's first childhood memory of food was eating porridge. 'Porridge every single day of my life as a child – and embellished only with salt... though I also recall a Haliborange Vitamin C tablet sitting on my porridge spoon every morning, too!'

Evelyn loved school dinners – the main weekday meal – and so tea at home was something simple like boiled eggs or corned beef sandwiches. But Sunday lunch was 'the only posh meal of the week', and for this meal there might be Scotch broth (soup served first then the meat and lots of vegetables after), or occasionally sirloin steaks or – and this was Evelyn's favourite – mince and tatties. The mince was flavoured with lots of vegetables such as peas, carrots and onions. Evelyn and her dad also added oatmeal to the mince, a habit the other members of her family eschewed. There was also always a sweet on Sundays, very often rhubarb crumble from garden rhubarb. Since her mum played the organ in church every Sunday, Evelyn and her dad also had to take charge of keeping an eye on the lunch as it cooked so that when the organist came home, lunch was ready.

Evelyn's mum made her own butter and cheese and Evelyn fondly recalls the cheese-making process: 'I regularly went to steal some of the soft salty curds, which I loved eating but was scolded for doing it every time.' Her mum also baked – sponges, Scotch pancakes (with their lovely smell) and chicken or beef pies, even though she never really enjoyed cooking or baking. It was just something a farmer's wife had to do.

There was nothing Evelyn really hated to eat as a child: 'There was no choice – if you didn't like something you went hungry.' In the summer the family would sometimes take the car out on a Sunday afternoon and perhaps stop on the way home for an ice cream, but this, as well as the occasional fish suppers, were the only time they ate out. Although, as she grew older, Evelyn remembers a new Indian restaurant in Ellon which served up (incongruously for the 1970s) haggis samosas.

The mention of stovies made Evelyn nostalgic, for she, like so many Scots, loved it. Often it would be made for a Sunday-night dish or Monday tea, using leftover meat from Sunday lunch or, if it was to be made quickly, corned beef. Any leftover stovies was also fried if and when hunger struck.

Another dish Evelyn fondly remembered was 'saps': hot milk with bread and sugar. 'This was made with milk straight from the cow, poured into a pan, white bread torn into it, then sugar added to taste. This was heated then eaten with a spoon. Saps were also eaten during summer in harvest time when the men were working on the farm all night; there was always soup on the go for them, but for immediate sustenance a pot of saps was also quickly rustled up.'

Cloutie dumpling was made at home for special occasions and she remembers her mum having to wash and dry the clout (cloth) after the dumpling was done. One other dish that she loved then and now was cabbage simply cooked with lots of black pepper and some butter. 'I was not a green-vegetable fan but absolutely loved a plate of cabbage.'

Evelyn loves Scottish food but, of course, can never recommend any restaurants in Scotland that serve proper Scottish food. 'Why on earth are our traditional and delicious dishes of stovies and mince and tatties never served in restaurants across the land?'

Mince and Tatties
serves 4

Sue says: Though Evelyn's mince is served with boiled potatoes, many prefer their potatoes mashed, so if you do, just mash them with some hot milk and a good dod of butter.

1 tbsp oil
1 large onion, peeled and finely chopped
450g/1 lb beef mince
2 medium carrots, peeled and sliced
1 tbsp toasted pinhead oatmeal

1 beef stock cube
salt and pepper, to taste
gravy granules/powder (Bisto if you
   can get it), or cornflour
450g/1 lb boiled potatoes (cooked)

Heat the oil in a pan and sauté the onion until it is browned. Add the mince and cook until well browned.

Drain off the liquid and add the carrots and oatmeal. Mix well and pour in enough water to just cover. Crumble in the stock cube, season and stir. Cover the pan and simmer the mince for about 20 minutes.

Once the mince is cooked, thicken it with about 3 teaspoons of gravy powder, or cornflour mixed with a little cold water. Serve the mince with boiled potatoes.

Dougray Scott, actor
born 1965

Just one chat with Dougray Scott and you can tell that food is hugely important to him. There are so many dishes from childhood that nowadays he still loves, both to eat and cook. One of his earliest memories was the family Sunday meal of brisket, as his dad was friendly with a butcher from Glasgow. He also recalls with great fondness Loch Fyne kippers, herring in oatmeal, and prawns. 'Being cold-water Scottish prawns, they are so much tastier than the larger warm-water prawns found elsewhere in the world.'

Arbroath Smokies are another favourite indeed, Dougray loved all fish and used to adore a treat of a fish supper at the Anstruther Fish Bar (he was brought up in Fife) which was followed by an 'Oyster' – wafer 'shells' which were half-chocolate/coconut coated and with mallow inside and filled with wonderful Italian ice cream.

Dougray's mum was a good cook – her rhubarb crumble just wonderful. 'It had the perfect combination of crispness and chewiness.' They grew rhubarb in the garden and as a boy he recalls washing it then dipping sticks into bowls of white sugar, like so many other Scots children.

His mum baked cakes such as chocolate sponge and scones, and he still recalls high tea at Dunblane Hydro on special occasions: their fabulous sponge cakes with red icing and coconut, and scones with cream and jam. His mum would also serve steamed sponge puddings which he remembers taking forever to prepare and then cook.

When he is back in Scotland, either visiting family or filming, one of the things Dougray craves, for both its taste and the fact it is so synonymous with childhood, is fruit dumpling fried for breakfast with eggs and sausages. 'But rather like the Scotch pies and bridies from my childhood, though I still love them, they are now only occasional treats as they are not exactly healthy.'

One food he would not crave, however, as he loathed it as a child, is potted hough, because of its gelatinous consistency. But he did love stovies and his mum's Monday hotpot made from leftover Sunday roast and the really good meatloaf his dad made in a cylindrical earthenware jar. His dad was also a dab hand at making egg nog, flavoured with just a tiny bit of brandy. When I asked if he was allowed to go to school with a faint glow of brandy, he told me it was just for treats and only ever at weekends!

Porridge is something Dougray still loves and makes often: he cooks his with milk and a little salt and eats it sprinkled with Demerara sugar and sliced bananas. His sweet tooth does not stretch as far as his dad's, though, who loved eating tablet and macaroon bars, which Dougray finds just too sweet; his favourite 'biscuit' nowadays is a Tunnock's Caramel Log.

Talk of school lunches brings back memories of 'Beasties' Graveyard and Custard', which, when he explained what it was, sounds to me like a combination of warm currant slice and Border tart. 'It was shortcrust pastry filled with raisins (the beasties!) and served with watery custard, which in fact I loved as it was like my mum's.'

Apart from his mum's mince and tatties, another great favourite was beef stew cooked overnight. He still loves to make it now.

Overnight Beef Stew

serves 6–8

My mum cooked this often, and it is one of my favourite dishes; she never added the peas but I reckon these make it my own signature dish.

flour, for coating
salt and pepper
1kg/2 lb 4 oz stewing beef (ask your
    butcher to cut some really good
    beef for you), cut into cubes
oil, for cooking
2 onions, peeled and chopped

4 carrots, peeled and chopped
2 leeks, chopped
1 small turnip (swede), peeled
    and chopped
600ml/1 pint fresh beef stock
Dijon mustard
couple of handfuls of frozen peas

Season some flour and place in a large plastic bag with the beef and shake well, to coat. Seal this in a hot pan with a little oil then remove.

Add the onions, carrots, leeks and turnip to the pan and sweat these down. Then transfer these and the meat to a big cast-iron pan. Cover with fresh beef stock, season well and stir in some Dijon mustard. Cover with a lid then place in a low oven, preheated to 150°C/300°F/Gas 2 for at least 4 hours, or overnight.

Once cooked, you can cool the stew then reheat it the next day when it is even better. Then add some frozen peas to the cooked hot stew, heat it until the peas are cooked, then serve it piping hot with some broccoli or French beans and new potatoes tossed in mint and butter.

A.L. Kennedy, novelist
and short-story writer
born 1965

Alison's earliest childhood food memory growing up in Dundee was eating bone marrow out of bones, which she loved. She also remembers eating rusks – and digestive biscuits with butter.

Her mother was a very good cook and taught her to bake and make sauces, and also pickled and made jam and marmalade and ice cream, and still does. Alison loves home-made bread, although she doesn't often have the time to make it herself and she misses it when she doesn't. She enjoys the whole process, saying it smells great and tastes infinitely better than shop-bought bread. She also remembers from her mum's kitchen proper apple pie, beef bourguignon and 'this laborious thing where my mother dipped orange segments in chocolate'; this latter she reckons she probably wouldn't like so much now, as she doesn't really have a sweet tooth.

As a child, Alison hated broccoli, because it always seemed to contain spiders – and she also didn't like fat, gristle, gravy, sauces or spices. Her grandpa scared her with oysters. She confesses she was a bit of a fussy eater. Despite this, she was taught to cook a bit of everything at home, and by the time she was a teenager her mother would cook the main course and she would do the baking, although she doesn't bake now at all, apart from bread.

She has always liked porridge, but the only dish Alison has ever cooked that she considers Scottish would be cullen skink, which she loves. She says that when she was growing up 'the idea of "Scottish food" didn't really exist – unless you meant broth, or pancakes, or oatcakes, or stovies (which seemed to mean almost anything: could be wonderful, could be horrific) or the horrible thing given at school instead of proper haggis. There wasn't really any sense that Scotland had a cuisine. It was all a bit low self-esteem in those days.'

She confesses she does not really get 'food homesickness' when abroad, although she believes that outside of India, Scotland has the best Indian food ever, so she misses curries when away. 'And potato scones, oddly!'

Alison's Christmas began early: her Great-uncle Edgar was a turkey farmer in Staffordshire and at Easter she would go down and pick out a turkey when she was a kid; she didn't quite understand that this would be bad news for the turkey, although she doesn't think he actually made a note and really sent them the one she pointed at! 'Either way,' she says, 'in December the family would all go to the Dundee railway station and this enormous corpse would be loaded out of the luggage van and that would be the Christmas turkey. It would get cleaned up in the bath and then we would eat it forever, which suited me because I liked turkey and all the bits and bobs with it – plus the home-made Christmas pudding and the home-made cake.'

Beef and Chestnut Stew
serves 4–5

You'll have to bear in mind that I never use recipes, I just make things up, but I do remember a beef and chestnut stew that my mother made and I make a version of it... The result is very rich, and goes well with good mash. And you tell me why I keep having to use European chestnuts when they grow in the UK and we do virtually nothing with them?

1 large onion
garlic cloves (as many as you like)
olive oil, for cooking
600g/1 lb 5 oz stewing steak
    (preferably organic), cubed
seasoned flour
500g/1 lb 2 oz cooked sweet
    chestnuts (you seem to only get
    them in 500g instalments)

dash of Worcestershire sauce
dash of Teriyaki sauce
ground allspice
ground cinnamon
enough good stock to cover

Take a large onion and as much garlic as you'd like (I like a lot). Soften them in a pan with some olive oil. Roll the cubed steak in seasoned flour then add it to the pan to seal. Transfer to a casserole (or you can cook on the stove top, but this may give you rubbery beef) with the chestnuts, a dash of Worcestershire sauce, a bit of Teriyaki sauce, some allspice, maybe some cinnamon and cover with a good stock. (I sometimes skip the flour rolling and thicken the stock with ground almonds at this point.) Cook in an oven preheated to 160°C/325°F/Gas 3 for 2–3 hours.

Ally McCoist, footballer
born 1962

Ally McCoist's earliest childhood food memory when growing up in the Bellshill area of Glasgow is of cereal: 'Cereal. Cereal, morning, noon and night. I can't even remember what variety, just cereal. And if anyone asked me what were my favourite childhood dishes, I'd say, cereal!'

His mum Jessie made soup, 'but only once and it wasn't as good as Gran's', he tells me. 'And I remember we had good steak pie on Hogmanay.

'My Aunt Bett is a good cook and she once owned a restaurant. The family didn't eat out much when I was young, unless it was at Aunt Bett's and it was free! But we did have fish suppers sometimes.'

There was nothing much that Ally hated to eat, 'apart from tomatoes as a kid; I'm fine with them now, though. And also I really struggled to masticate dough balls.

'I never learned to cook as a child, though I am quite handy now with pasta or a curry. I have even passed the "kids' test": they like Dad's cooking. But as for cooking Scottish dishes, unfortunately the Scottish dishes usually come in the form of ready-made from a well-known food outlet!

'If I've been out of the country, when I return home to Scotland I like nothing better than that old traditional – well for me anyway – Scottish curry. But there is one Scottish dish that, although not summing up my childhood, I am very partial to these days: steak Balmoral.'

Steak Balmoral

serves 4

Sue says: **Here is my recipe for this classic dish.**

4 Aberdeen Angus steaks
   (preferably rib-eye)
olive oil
25g/1 oz butter
300g/10½ oz mushrooms, thinly sliced

salt and pepper, to taste
4 tbsp Scotch whisky
200ml/7 fl oz crème fraîche
2 tbsp Worcestershire sauce
1 tbsp coarse grain mustard

Bring the steaks to room temperature and place them on a plate with a smear of olive oil. Heat the butter and a little olive oil in the pan and gently fry the mushrooms until tender, then remove. Return the heat to high, season the steaks, then fry until done to your liking, turning once. Remove to a warm plate.

Increase the heat, add the whisky, bubble away for a minute, stirring, then add the crème fraîche, Worcestershire sauce and mustard and bubble away until thick. Season to taste. Using a slotted spoon, return the mushrooms to the pan (discarding any liquor), then serve with the steaks. Serve with mashed potatoes and spinach.

Barbara Dickson, singer
born 1947

Barbara Dickson can vividly remember her Granny Dickson's chocolate Viennas from her childhood. These were kept in a tin in the top of Granny's press. When she went to visit her with Alastair, her brother, they were given one each as a special treat.

Relating how important food was as she grew up in Dunfermline, she tells me, 'My mum didn't cook much, that I remember. My father was a good cook and made plain fare and fantastic chips. We usually ate mince and tatties, steak pie and boiled potatoes and peas or cabbage. My mum could bake, though, and we had apple pies and suet puddings in the winter.'

She says she still likes nice chips, but 'they're usually disgusting these days. My dad's were brown and like doorsteps, so I still like those "posh" chips you can be served in restaurants which come in a pile neatly stacked like my dad's chips. I also love Scottish macaroon and tablet hugely. I try to buy them when I'm home.'

The family never ate out, as nobody did in those days. 'We only visited people and had a cup of tea and a slice of cake.' But on occasional treats at the chip shop, Barbara enjoyed both fish suppers and pudding suppers, but she liked the haggis suppers best.

She hated liver as a child and her mother used to give her and her brother cod liver oil, floating on bionic orange juice she got somewhere to 'build us up'. (Barbara says they just spat it out.)

As for Scottish food that she enjoys these days, 'I love Atholl Brose [an oatmeal, whisky and honey concoction], I'm crazy about raspberries and I love haggis, but I don't make it. I usually buy it from a good supplier down here in England. I love Scottish breakfast rolls and good smoked salmon and malt whisky... in fact, everything apart from deep-fried Mars Bars!'

She also likes to eat Arbroath Smokies, finnan haddies and anything that is local to wherever she is.

Barbara loved Hogmanay as a child because it was one night on which they were allowed to stay up late. 'I remember Black Bun and ginger wine, home-made steak pies and stovies (glorious) with mutton fat and a little meat, but not much – probably all to soak up the alcohol.'

Steak Pie

serves 6

Sue says: The pie Barbara remembers from New Year was home-made steak pie in a metal pie dish full to the brim with glossy steak with a pie funnel in the centre, covered with yummy puff pastry. This is my version.

50g/1¾ oz dripping or butter
900g/2 lb stewing beef, diced
45g/1½ oz plain flour, seasoned
1 large onion, peeled and chopped
4 large carrots, peeled and cut into
    thick slices

600ml/1 pint beef stock, hot
1 heaped tbsp tomato purée
1 tbsp Worcestershire sauce
salt and pepper, to taste
225g/8 oz ready-rolled puff pastry
1 small free-range egg, beaten

Heat the dripping or butter in a heavy saucepan or casserole. Toss half the meat in the well-seasoned flour, add it to the pan and brown it all over. When browned, remove it with a slotted spoon, coat the remaining meat and brown this batch all over.

Remove with a slotted spoon and add the onion and carrots (if you need it, add a little extra fat at this stage). Gently fry until softened, for about 5 minutes, then return the meat to the pan with the hot stock, tomato purée and Worcestershire sauce. Grind in plenty of black pepper and some salt, stir well and bring to the boil. Cover and reduce to a simmer. Cook very gently for 2 hours, stirring once, then check the seasoning, tip into a 1.8 litre/3 pint pie dish and allow to cool completely. Refrigerate overnight.

Next day, cut a long strip of the rolled-out pastry. Wet your fingers lightly and dampen the edges of the pie dish. Place the pastry strip around the rim of the pie dish, then brush with the beaten egg. Place the remaining pastry over the top as a lid and press down to seal all the edges. Trim off any excess pastry and crimp the edges between thumb and forefinger. Brush with beaten egg and snip a hole – with scissors – in the middle.

Bake in an oven preheated to 220°C/425°F/Gas 7 for 30–35 minutes until puffed up and golden brown. You might need to lightly lay a piece of foil over the surface for the last 10 minutes or so to prevent burning. Serve piping hot.

Sally Magnusson, broadcaster
born 1955

Food was never hugely important in itself when Sally Magnusson was growing up in Glasgow. Although her mother made sure they had one good hot meal a day, she would be the last person to claim to be any great shakes in the kitchen. 'Mum was a career girl reporter before she got married, more proficient at rustling up an article than a scone.' Indeed, Sally describes one unforgettable incident in the Magnusson household: 'Sure enough, her pioneering attempt at baking a cake for my first birthday ended in disaster. She put the icing on – and then gaily placed the cake in the oven. I suppose we can be grateful she hadn't lit the candles as well.'

But there were also successful dishes: 'I used to love stovies, made with layers of potatoes, leftover meat or tinned corned beef and onions. All gooey and hot and delicious.' Another favourite she told me about were egg pieces, a favourite teatime meal – bread dipped in a mixture of egg and milk and then fried. Indeed, Sally's children still enjoy that one. 'I remember being quite keen on Creamola Foam for a while, too; I'm sure it must have been unbelievably disgusting, but it felt like the height of sophistication. And those strange little Dairylea cheese triangles were always fun (spread on a slice of purest white plain loaf, naturally). Oh, and toast smeared with thick black treacle was a favourite for breakfast: if you were to present me with that today, with a big mug of tea, I would be in seventh heaven.'

Fish suppers were a great treat as a child – all wrapped up in newspaper and drenched with vinegar – but Sally also recalls the downside of growing up in the 1950s and 1960s: 'I can still remember my horror at the sight, and smell, and touch, and taste of tripe. It made me feel sick. I toyed with it once, managed a mouthful and then absolutely refused. Even thinking about the long, white sliminess of it now makes me want to retch. Spam wasn't great shakes either, particularly the round kind dotted with little white bits. Heaven knows what these white bits were.'

Like her mother, Sally modestly says she is never going to win any prizes for cuisine. 'But although I say so myself, I'm rather good at lentil broth. And my mince and tatties are justly famed for being more or less edible.'

Stovies

serves 4

This is a recipe for stovies (stoved potatoes) as my mother used to make it and as I occasionally tried on my children when they were young enough not to complain. Actually, it's delicious.

500g/1 lb 2 oz potatoes
1 large onion, peeled
1 carrot, peeled (optional)
1 small turnip (swede), peeled (optional)

approx. 200g/7 oz corned beef or leftover meat
a few tablespoons of stock
salt and pepper, to taste

Chop the potatoes and cut the onion into rings. Add some thickly chopped carrot and turnip, too, if you feel like it. Place these in a big pot between layers of corned beef and any leftover meat and stock from the Sunday roast. (Some people use dripping here.) Keep piling up the layers until you reach the top of the pan. Add a little hot water, put the lid on tight and cook slowly for about 35 minutes or until the potatoes are tender. Season with salt and pepper.

This is bringing back such mouth-watering memories that I intend to cook it again immediately. What have I been missing all these years?

Annabel Goldie, politician, Leader of the Scottish Conservatives in the Scottish Parliament
born 1950

Annabel Goldie's first food memory is of porridge; not served with the traditional salt, but with sugar, 'and sometimes with golden syrup'. Growing up in Renfrewshire, she was surrounded by delicious food as her mum was a good cook and so were her aunts.

Her favourite childhood foods were mince and mashed potatoes: 'We were allowed to flatten and plough the mashed potatoes with our forks. We also enjoyed "Big Omnibus Salad" [her family name for a massive, all-encompassing salad] made with vegetables from the garden. And for pudding, oven-baked rice pudding with raspberry jam and Queen of Puddings.'

She had fish and chips from the chip shop only as a special treat, but she would always opt to take a fish supper home rather than eating outside.

Annabel learned to cook the basics at home: scrambled eggs, omelette, casseroles, scones and white sauce, and nowadays she loves to cook many Scottish things. She will cook: 'Scottish lamb in any form you like and also local beef. Over the winter, I make porridge. And, quite often, I make oatmeal potatoes by putting a little butter in the boiled potatoes, covering them with oatmeal and leaving them on the heat briefly to warm through. I also love haddock and kippers.'

Christmas Day and New Year's Day were special in her family and they tended to have – if not turkey – pheasant or goose. Roast chicken was popular at other times of the year, her mother stuffing it with breadcrumbs, butter, finely chopped onion and about two tablespoons of finely chopped parsley. The chicken in cider recipe here is another family favourite.

Chicken in Cider
serves 4

4 chicken joints or fillets on the bone
seasoned plain flour
1 onion, peeled and chopped

butter and oil
1 litre bottle of cider (I prefer sweet
   to dry) – you won't need it all

Coat the chicken pieces in the seasoned flour.

Soften the onion by frying it in a mixture of butter and oil, then tip it into an ovenproof casserole dish.

Remove the chicken from the flour, shaking off any excess, but keeping the extra flour. Brown the chicken pieces in butter and oil and add them to the casserole dish. Add some of the leftover seasoned flour to the frying pan to make a brown roux before adding enough of the cider to make a sauce (stir it continuously to keep it smooth). Pour the sauce over the chicken in the casserole dish.

Put the covered dish in an oven preheated to 180°C/350°F/Gas 4 for 1 hour and 15 minutes, but check during cooking to see how it's getting on. The chicken is ready when the flesh is tender and lifting off the bone.

Elaine C. Smith, actor
born 1958

'As a toddler I remember loving egg custard with rice from those wee baby tins and I still love the taste of rusks. When I was older, as a kid, it was caramel custard; my mum used to make it and I loved it. I think I have just found the source of my sweet tooth!' Elaine C. Smith laughs as she recalls her earliest childhood food memories.

She goes on to tell me about the importance of food at their home near Motherwell: 'Food was love in our house and at my gran's. My gran always set a very formal dining table with napkins and stuff. Every day. When we were in the house we spent most of our time at the kitchen table. My mum was a good cook but was actually taught by my dad, who at eighty still makes his soups, stews, steak and mushrooms and curries every other day. My mum was a great baker and her lemon meringue pie was a star turn.'

Saturday night was a treat for them, with sirloin steak, onions, mushrooms in gravy with chips. Elaine's dad made this every week and it was followed by a Galbraith's cream cookie, which, according to Elaine, was heaven.

They only ate out very rarely, as there just weren't the places to go and, besides, they couldn't afford it. So eating out was a real treat and tended to be on special days out or holidays – but even then Elaine's dad was a great one for the picnic or the outdoor fry-up at the side of the road. 'If we did eat out, it was a fish tea in Whitley Bay or Morecambe.'

As a child, she always hated Brussels sprouts and turnip, which of course now she likes.

Hogmanay was when her dad made his exotic chicken curry: 'I'm sure he got it off the back of a Vesta packet, because it had raisins, sultanas, the lot in it. We thought it was the most exotic thing on the planet. Well, it was 1972!'

Elaine learned to cook at home and loved helping her mum bake (just to get to lick the bowl!) and her dad taught her to cook the steaks that Elaine's husband and children wolf down now. She also still makes childhood dishes such as soup – in particular lentil soup and vegetable soups, always favourites for the winter. Her children love haggis and neeps too, even though Elaine had never tasted haggis until she was an adult.

Roast Chicken for Sunday Dinner
serves 4–6

We used to walk to the local Lanarkshire farm and buy the chicken for this recipe; they literally went out to the shed and wrung its neck and we had to walk home with it!

My dad plucked it because we thought it was too gross and then my mum washed it, and prepared it like this:

1 whole chicken
sage and onion stuffing
approx. 25g/1 oz butter, for greasing
salt and pepper, to taste

about 1 tsp of mixed herbs
3 rashers bacon
baby potatoes

Place the chicken in a dish lined with foil (large enough to wrap the bird in). Put the sage and onion stuffing inside the carcass. Use butter to grease the top of the bird, then season with salt and black pepper and some mixed herbs. Place the bacon rashers across the top of the chicken, too. Surround the chicken with baby potatoes within the foil then loosely wrap the whole lot up in the foil.

Place the dish in an oven preheated to 180°C/350°F/Gas 4 and cook according to weight (around 20 mins per 450g/1 lb). For the last 30 minutes, open the foil and allow the roast to brown. Ensure it's cooked by checking the juices run clear when the thickest part of the flesh is pierced with a skewer. Lovely!

Jason White, rugby player
born 1978

'Because my granny and grandpa were butchers in Melrose, I was told that as a child I was fed on minced steak; my mum would come home after visiting them with fillet steaks which she would mince for me. Nothing but the best!'

Jason White lived in Burntisland in Fife until he was eight, then moved to Aberdeen where he stayed until he was seventeen. His first childhood memory of food was of eating his granny's chocolate cake when he went to visit them in Melrose. Food was important in his home, as his mum and gran were excellent cooks, both preparing everything from scratch. He recalls being at primary school and walking home for lunch and sitting eating with his mum and dad at the kitchen table. But sometimes, as a special treat, he would have school dinners – of which his abiding memory is bright pink custard with steamed pudding.

During his time in Burntisland Jason remembers there being a routine to everyday fare, so mince and tatties would be on the menu on a certain day every week. Once served up, Jason told me, 'I would then mash it all up and make it into "Bin Hill", which is the name of a hill at the back of Burntisland' – so he would shape it into a fetching hillock then, handywork admired briefly, devour it.

Jason says he was a typical boy with regards to food and ate everything put in front of him, but remembers certain dishes most fondly, his mum's chocolate pudding (a sort of chocolate custard) in particular. He also remembers having the treat of a fish supper every Wednesday night on the way home after swimming. Fish was popular in their family, and when the fish van called, once a week, Jason's mum would buy white fish which she would bread herself then fry and serve. Nowadays he likes healthy food and eschews anything deep-fried, if at all possible.

However, Jason does admit to less healthy habits at mid-morning break when he was at secondary school in Aberdeen. 'We would all go to the big canteen and the choice there was either yum yums [a sweet pastry/doughnut] or rowies [Aberdeen butteries] which were sitting under the hot plate. I liked the less-sweet option. And every Sunday Dad would bring home a bag of rowies, which we would heat in the oven then eat smeared with butter. Not exactly healthy, but delicious.'

The only thing he truly hated as a child was Brussels sprouts, but luckily they were only served at Christmas time.

One of his favourite dishes nowadays is a haggis-stuffed chicken, which he and his wife Bev had once cooked for his mum and dad. His parents then took it a stage further and added dried fruits. The result is a superb and original roast chicken dish that is the White family's speciality.

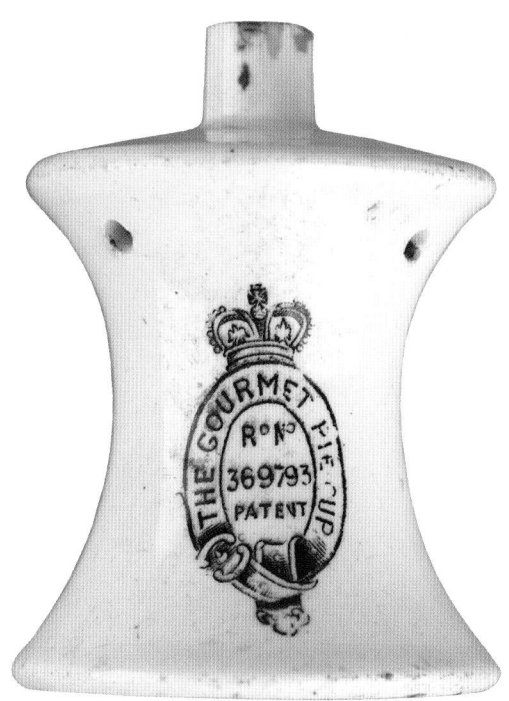

Haggis-stuffed Chicken
serves 6

1 large oven-ready chicken
½ butcher's haggis

a large handful of chopped dried apricots, dates and prunes, and some sultanas

I take one large chicken then about half a haggis (I usually buy a Macsweens at the airport on the way back south to England) and heat it through a little so it is easier to handle. I then mix the apricots, dates and prunes, with the sultanas, combine all these with the haggis and stuff this into the chicken.

Then I roast the chicken in an oven preheated to 180°C/350°F/Gas 4 and cook according to its weight (around 20 minutes per 450g/1 lb), giving it a little longer since it is stuffed. Serve the cooked chicken with broccoli and roast carrots, roast parsnips and – my favourite – roast sweet potatoes.

William Patey, HM Ambassador
(Saudi Arabia, Iraq, Sudan)
born 1953

William Patey's earliest memory of food is a negative one: of being made to eat tripe as a young boy when staying with his auntie. He told me, 'I can still visualise it now – a pale skin which looked like chicken soaked in a milky substance.'

Cooking for pleasure was not a big part of his life growing up in Leith, Edinburgh, with his parents working long hours, so convenience food was more usually served up than home-cooked dishes. The exception was Sunday, when they would enjoy a more traditional roast.

Nowadays he loves haggis, neeps and tatties and still craves this traditional Scottish dish. Given the amount of time he spends outside the country, especially in Arab and Islamic countries, it is never available locally, so he looks forward to the annual Caledonian or Burns Nights when haggis is flown in especially from Macsweens in Edinburgh. It is usually served as an appetiser, so when everyone else is tentatively taking small helpings he likes to pile his plate high and skip the subsequent main course. William loves the spiciness of the haggis, and the lovely blend of flavours when mixed with the neeps and tatties.

At university in Dundee in the early 1970s, William lived above a fish and chip shop on the Blackness Road and virtually survived on white pudding suppers, which were, of course, much cheaper than the more usual fish suppers. As a student, he never progressed beyond cooking 'the survival spaghetti Bolognese' that he learned to make at university.

These days, something he loves to prepare for special occasions is Atholl Brose, served as an aperitif for St Andrew's Night. The combination of water soaked in oats, whisky, Drambuie, cream and honey is, according to William, 'just fantastic, if a little rich. It is an amazing stomach liner for what usually turns into an evening of heavy drinking.'

William's dad, who is English but has lived in Scotland for fifty-six years, still makes a mean Scotch broth in the winter. When William was growing up, he would make a huge pot of it and the family would eat it for days. And Bill told me 'the warmth and comfort of that soup sums up my childhood. But haggis, neeps and tatties remains my favourite dish. Although we used to buy our haggis direct from the butcher rather than make it. As a child I loved to mash it all together into a mountain.'

Haggis, Neeps and Tatties
serves 4–6

Sue says: This is my traditional haggis, neeps and tatties recipe for William.

1 butcher's haggis

For the tatties:
1kg/2 lb 4 oz floury potatoes
100g/3½ oz butter

100ml/3½ fl oz full-fat milk, hot
salt and pepper, to taste

For the neeps:
750g/1 lb 10 oz turnip (swede; approx.
   1 large turnip)
50g/1¾ oz butter

salt and pepper, to taste
nutmeg, to grate

To heat your haggis (remember it has already been cooked), wrap it in foil and reheat in an oven preheated to 180°C/450°F/Gas 4 for approximately 45 minutes per 450g/1 lb.

For the tatties, peel then cut the potatoes and cook in a pan of boiling, salted water until tender. For the neeps, peel the turnip and cut into chunks. Boil in another pan of salted boiling water for about 20 minutes or until tender. When done, drain the potatoes and the neeps well and return each to their respective pans to thoroughly dry over a low heat, shaking the pan often.

To finish the potatoes, add the butter and mash with a potato masher, then add the hot milk and mash again, tasting and adding salt and pepper accordingly. Add the butter to the neeps and mash, add salt, pepper and grated nutmeg to taste. Cut open the haggis and serve it all together, piping hot.

Allan Little, broadcaster
born 1959

Allan Little was brought up in a village in Galloway that had only five hundred inhabitants but, surprisingly, two butcher's shops. Most of his fondest memories of food are therefore of meat and game (his grandfather was a gamekeeper), including, of course, mince and potatoes.

Allan also vividly recalls the joy of being out fishing with his father and brother when he was about ten and his brother catching a rainbow trout. 'My father gutted it on the spot then cooked it on a slate over a fire. I remember first the beautiful colours of the trout before eating it, then the fabulous vivid pink colour of the flesh once the skin had been removed.' Since this memory was so special, he reckons it spoils all his adult experiences in fish restaurants, as nothing can ever match that trout.

His grandmother was a great baker, making everything on the iron girdle (griddle): from potato scones to soda scones and pancakes. She won many prizes at the SWRI (Scottish Women's Rural Institute) fair in Dunragit, where they lived, for her legendary gingerbread, sponge cakes, shortbread and scones. 'Anything involving flour, butter and eggs she was good at,' says Allan. 'And she was also a dab hand at jams, made from garden-grown rhubarb or wild brambles that we would be sent to gather.' He recalls vividly the sight and also the sweet smell from the jeely bag inverted over a stool, dripping the bright purple bramble jelly; and seeing rows upon rows of jam and jellies in jars in the cold pantry.

His grandmother also reared turkeys, pigs, and geese and chickens for their eggs, which Allan and his siblings (there were four of them) would be sent to collect. Perhaps slightly unusually for a Scots child, roast pheasant was the norm in their house, given his grandfather's job (they lived only three miles away), and so his grandmother knew precisely how to cook it – as it is a game bird that can dry out so easily. He recalls 'the sensation of finding bits of lead shot in my mouth from the birds, but most of all I remember the fine flavour and texture of these delicious roast birds'.

Roast Pheasant
serves 4

Sue says: I have added optional extras (gin, jelly and crème fraîche) to my roast pheasant recipe to make a delicious sauce. I am not sure, however, Allan's grandmother would have approved as Allan told me neither she nor his grandfather drank.

75g/2¾ oz butter
5–6 juniper berries

2 medium or 1 large oven-ready
    pheasant
salt and pepper, to taste

For the sauce:
150ml/5 fl oz gin
2 tbsp redcurrant jelly

200ml/7 fl oz crème fraîche

Heat the butter in a frying pan then crush the juniper berries with a pestle and mortar and add them to the pan. Once hot, add the pheasant or pheasants and brown all over – about 5 minutes.

Remove them to a roasting tin and pour over the melted butter. Season with salt and pepper. Place in an oven preheated to 220°C/400°F/Gas 6 for 40–50 minutes, depending on the weight of the pheasant/s. Baste well every 10–15 minutes. When cooked, remove to a board, cover with foil and rest for 10–15 minutes, before carving into thin slices.

For the sauce, spoon off most of the fat from the roasting tin, leaving about 1 tablespoon. Set the tin directly onto the stove over a medium heat. Pour in the gin (carefully if you are using gas, it might ignite) then stir well to scrape up all the caramelised bits.

Let it bubble away for about 5 minutes until reduced by half, then lower the heat and add the jelly. Stir until dissolved then add the crème fraîche. Stir well, increase the heat again and bubble for 2–3 minutes. Season to taste, strain into a jug and serve with the pheasant.

Tavish Scott, Leader of the Scottish Liberal Democrats
born 1966

Brought up in Shetland on a farm on the island of Bressay, over the sea from Lerwick, Tavish has fond memories of good home-cooked food, but in particular of Shetland lamb. His family farmed native breeds of sheep which fed on seaweed, rough grazing and heather, and the flavour of the resulting lamb is superb and quite unique. Tavish reckoned he never appreciated just how good Shetland lamb was until he left home; he seldom orders lamb in restaurants now, for fear of disappointment.

Although he now adores fish, meat was the mainstay of his diet when growing up on one of the most remote islands in Scotland. Beef and lamb were most often served, accompanied by vegetables grown in the garden by Tavish's mum. His mum was also a dab hand at soups, and one in particular – reestit mutton and tattie soup – brings back fond memories. Reestit mutton is cured mutton, salted for some ten days then hung up on hooks to dry, traditionally suspended over the peat fire. Although it is sold at the Lerwick butchers, it is more common for people to cure their own, so many houses would have a piece of reestit mutton hanging up in the kitchen. Tavish nowadays not only loves the soup but also loves cutting thin slices from the mutton to eat alone or with bread. Who needs Parma ham when we in Scotland have reestit mutton?

Reestit mutton soup was also the dish, accompanied by 'floorie' (wheat) bannocks, that was, and still is, served at the Shetlanders' renowned January celebrations Up Helly Aa. (Beremeal bannocks are also served, but bere is more typical in Orkney.) Tavish remembers being allowed to go over in the boat to Lerwick for Up Helly Aa but 'only once I was thirteen, for there is more than a little drinking involved! Hence the bannocks and soup to soak it up.'

He also remembers strawberries, raspberries and most of all rhubarb from the garden, all converted into wonderful, if rather runny, jam. There was also junket made from the milk from their own cow (Daisy), which was unpasteurised and served with garden fruit such as stewed rhubarb.

And of course, like all other Scottish homes, there was always home-made cake in the tins, lemon cake being one of his particular favourites.

Whenever Tavish returns to Shetland from Edinburgh he still adores eating local lamb, but he is more and more partial to fish. A favourite is monkfish tails, but he also loves Shetland salmon, fresh or smoked. A good fish supper is still an occasional treat, as there is a chip shop with the freshest fish possible (two minutes from the harbour where it is landed) beside Tavish's Lerwick office. He told me, 'A fish supper was also the treat I enjoyed as a teenager when I had stayed too late after football practice and had missed the last ferry home to Bressay.'

Another local dish he enjoys still is sassermeat (a spiced sausagemeat which non-Shetlanders often deem an acquired taste!) fried with onions. But one of his favourites, both then and now, is that Scottish staple, good old mince and tatties.

Shetland Roast Lamb
serves 6–8

Sue says: Tavish's mum would produce simple roast lamb from the farm, with roast potatoes and garden vegetables such as carrots, red cabbage and kale – the latter loathed by Tavish as a child. This is my recipe for one of Tavish's favourite dishes.

1 large leg of lamb (approx. 2.5–3kg/ 5 lb 8 oz–6 lb 8 oz)
slivers of garlic and sprigs of rosemary (optional)

olive oil
sea salt and freshly ground black pepper, to taste

Set the lamb in a roasting tin. Insert slivers of garlic and rosemary all over, if you like. Drizzle with a little oil. Season with sea salt and freshly ground pepper.

Roast in an oven preheated to 220°C/425°F/Gas 7 for 20 minutes, then reduce the heat to 190°C/375°F/Gas 5 and continue to cook for 20 minutes per 450g/1 lb, basting a couple of times during cooking. Remove to a carving board, cover with foil and rest for 15–20 minutes while you make the gravy in the roasting tin. Serve with garden vegetables.

Alistair Darling, Chancellor of the Exchequer
born 1953

Although Alistair Darling's first memory of food was the morning ritual of brose-making in Stornoway (coarse oatmeal was put into a bowl, a tablespoon of sugar added with a large pinch of salt and a dod of butter, then boiling water stirred in before being eaten at once), his mother's memory was different. She recalls her baby son being held under one arm by her mother, his Granny Maclean, who was cooking kippers with her other arm while feeding the just-weaned baby some of the cured fish. The smoky flavour from this fish was 'enhanced' by the roaring fire only a few steps away from the Raeburn where she was cooking. Alistair's mother, who had been trying to raise her baby 'by the book', was not best pleased!

Although, as Alistair told me over tea served with his wife Maggie's delicious home-baked cakes, he moved all over the country because of his father's job, his fondest and most regular childhood memories were of their frequent visits to his mother's home of the Hebridean island of Lewis, where many aunts and cousins lived. The family still have a blackhouse (the traditional Lewis house) on Bernera; this is where Auntie Morag, another fantastic baker, made fabulous cakes, although another auntie, Auntie Nessie, also made the best chocolate cake and 'Lancashire Nuts' (two light, short, buttery biscuits sandwiched with butter cream and jam). These were so delicious and loved by the whole family that Maggie said we ought to rename them 'Auntie Nessie's Nuts'.

'While on Bernera', Alistair told me, 'I remember eating herring in oatmeal as there was so much herring landed in Stornoway harbour then: the fish was fried in oatmeal and I can still recall the taste of the soft flesh contrasting so well with the crumbly outer coating. I also fished for mackerel with my cousins and was so proud when I caught my first brown trout, but my mother gave it away to the neighbour so I never got to eat it! I remember cloutie dumpling, roast lamb and, probably best of all, the "*marags*" [the Gaelic for black pudding is "*marag dhubh*"], fried for breakfast perhaps with eggs from hens my granny kept. Thankfully, Stornoway black pudding can be bought all over Scotland now.'

He also remembers the Lewis Sunday roast (always lamb) with wonderful roast potatoes, peas and cabbage; and Crowdie, the fresh 'crofter's' cheese which his granny made. 'The crowdie was eaten on oatcakes which were freshly baked on the girdle [griddle]. My Lewis granny always baked her scones on the girdle, but my other granny, who was from Dundee, baked hers in the oven.'

Another Lewis speciality that he recalls seeing, but never tasting, is guga. These are plump young gannets harvested every year on a remote island forty miles north of Lewis, following a tradition that has continued for over four centuries. It entails a group of men – all from the north of Lewis – spending a fortnight catching the birds, which involves remarkable skills of rock-climbing, usually amid adverse weather conditions. Once killed, the birds are decapitated, plucked, singed, dewinged, then split and salted. When the men return home to Ness, in the north of the island, with their harvest, they are met on the quay by locals queuing to buy pairs of guga which will be desalinated, boiled and eaten with potatoes. When I told Alistair I had cooked and eaten guga (but thankfully only once!) he said he remembers many tales from his childhood, not just about their 'acquired' taste but also their vile and lingering smell!

Onto more pleasing odours, as Alistair described how his granny and aunts made their cakes without a wooden spoon, only using their hands. The method was not like rubbing in for crumbles or pastry, using the tips of your fingers, but creaming together the butter and eggs with whole hands, similar to the way Italian women combine flour and eggs for pasta. When Maggie tried to recreate Auntie Nessie's famous chocolate cake, she despaired that she could not get it as good until she realised it was because of the temperature. On Lewis, the butter and eggs would be ambient temperature (no fridges then) and because she used her hands to work the mixture, the warmth would also affect the final texture. For 'Nessie's Nuts', Auntie Nessie used to cream equal quantities of butter and flour with a third of the weight of both icing sugar and custard powder, bake them as little biscuits, then sandwich them together with butter cream icing and jam. And as I sat in Alistair Darling's garden eating more than my polite share of these, I thought, how fortunate to have family recipes handed down for posterity.

Lamb and Black Pudding Casserole
serves 8

My wife Maggie says, 'This is based on an old navarin of lamb recipe I've used forever, and adapted as the seasons change. Keep a check on the liquid levels. If it's looking too dry, add some water. In winter I've added cooked butter beans instead of new tatties, which makes it lovely and mealie.'

1kg/2 lb 4 oz lamb gigot (leg) chops
1 tbsp flour
2 onions, chopped small
olive oil, for cooking
2 leeks, sliced
1 tsp sugar
200ml/7 fl oz/1 cup wine
400g tin chopped tomatoes or a large
   jar of passata

2 large carrots, peeled and sliced
   (or in summer, 2 handfuls of small
   whole carrots)
1 bay leaf
a couple of sprigs of fresh thyme
   (or 1 tsp dried)
salt and pepper, to taste
8 small new potatoes, sliced thickly
8 slices of Stornoway black pudding
(skinned)
chopped parsley or coriander, to serve

Cut the gigot chops into pieces and toss them in the flour. In an ovenproof casserole, fry off the onions gently in olive oil until softening. Add the leeks and sweat until they are a tangled mass. Remove to a plate. Turn up the heat and brown the lamb in batches. Stir in the sugar, return the onions and leeks to the pan, then stir in the wine and wait until it bubbles. Add the tomatoes or passata. If using old carrots, add them now. Bring to the boil, add the bay leaf and thyme and season to taste. Cook slowly with a lid on the casserole for about 30 minutes – the timing really depends on the age of the lamb – or put it into an oven preheated to 170°C/ 325°F/Gas 3 for about the same length of time.

Remove the lid and add the sliced potatoes (and small carrots in summer). Put back on the hob or in the oven for another 30 minutes.

Meanwhile, place the sliced black pudding on a baking tray in the oven for 15 minutes. The outside will crisp up. Cut into large chunks and add it to the casserole for the last 15 minutes of cooking time.

I strew chopped parsley or coriander on top before serving. It's a really good one-pot meal in the summer. In winter I sometimes omit the new potatoes and serve it with mash.

Sue says: I have also strewn it with rocket instead of parsley or coriander and it works very well.

Hardeep Singh Kohli, broadcaster and writer
born 1969

Hardeep Singh Kohli's first memory of food was his mum's lamb curry. Sometimes there was chicken curry, but whichever it was, it was his job, aged about four, to taste it to see if it was cooked. 'This was in the days before pressure cookers, and so meat took ages to cook. I would also see if the chilli and salt were sufficient. I loved being in the kitchen!'

Food was of great significance in their family as Hardeep's life outside and inside the house were so different: 'I lived in duality: at home it was delicious Indian food, outside were school dinners which were not good at all and I hated them. My mum cooked everything from scratch and often my granny would look after us too and I used to help her cook. My granny's daal was the best; it is, after all, the heart of Punjabi food. I would watch her prepare the lentils then temper the oils, add spices and onions then taste for the perfect flavour.'

His mum also made some Scottish food – fish and chips, apple pie, mince pie. Her mince and tatties bore no resemblance to the dish most Scots were brought up on; hers was curried mince (cooked with cardamom, cumin, cinnamon sticks and bay) and with potatoes cooked in the actual mince. He loved all vegetables from okra and cabbage to bitter gourds, whereas his older brother would eat none, so his mum used to make vegetable soup so that he would at least eat some vegetables. One of his favourite dishes was bitter gourd ('*karela*') cooked in two ways: either stuffed with cooked spiced mince, sewn back up then cooked and served like stuffed marrow, or the gourd was stuffed with spices and the vegetable was then cooked in the mince. 'I know my DNA is most definitely Punjabi because I absolutely love dishes made of bitter gourd!'

As a family they rarely ate out, except on his dad's birthday when they usually went somewhere serving great Tandoori food (no-one had Tandoor ovens at home). But they would also have the occasional treat of fish suppers which Hardeep loves. 'When I was up north recently I had a morning roll filled with bacon and a tattie scone; no other country overloads so much on carbohydrates, does it?'

His dad also cooked and had a real passion for it. He would do plain roast chicken (unusually, no spices) but anything exotic, he was up for. Hardeep reckons that as far as cooking is concerned he acquired his skills from his mum, his flair from his granny and his ambitiousness from his dad. He loves to cook Scottish dishes to which he adds a twist: he cooks haggis, or cock-a-leekie soup (his daughter's favourite) developed into a thick stew, not unlike a pot-au-feu. He also loves experimenting with other Scottish dishes. One he is fiddling with is a stovies dish cooked in goose fat and served with veal mince or foie gras! But it is his mum's curries that not only sum up his childhood but also the dishes he loves cooking most.

Lamb Curry
serves 6–8

1kg/2 lb 4 oz lamb (any cut, but shoulder is my favourite)
500g/1 lb 2 oz onions, chopped
2 or 3 cloves of garlic, chopped
2.5cm/1 in piece of root ginger, peeled and chopped
green chillies (no fewer than two, no more than a dozen), seeded and chopped
salt
½ tsp turmeric

¼ tsp red chilli powder
½ tsp coriander powder
½ tsp ground cumin
3 tbsp corn or sunflower oil
potatoes, peeled and cut into chunks (optional)
400g tin chopped tomatoes
½ tsp garam masala
chopped fresh coriander leaves

Wash the meat well. Put it in a pot on a low heat. Add the onions, garlic, ginger and chillies. Mix well. Add the salt, turmeric, red chilli powder, coriander powder and cumin. Mix all together well and cook slowly, covered, on a low heat. The lamb should cook gently and slowly in its own juices for about 1½–2 hours or until it is tender.

When the meat is tender, add the cooking oil. (The chunks of potatoes can be added at this point and cooked before the tomatoes are added.) Increase the heat and add the chopped tomatoes. (You can add water having cooked the tomatoes if you like more sauce.) Cook the tomatoes well. Test the meat. When it is cooked, take the pot off the heat and add the garam masala and chopped coriander leaves.

puddings

Ewan McGregor, actor
born 1971

Ewan McGregor's earliest memories as a child are of eating Scotch pies with his dad while watching the rugby on television. The pies came with gravy and tomato sauce.

Some of the dishes he loved most in his childhood were his mum's beef and Guinness stew, her mince and potatoes and also her tablet. She was – and is – a great cook.

One of Ewan's favourite recipes is his mum's very special bread and butter pudding.

Bread and Butter Pudding
serves 6

butter, for greasing
8 slices of bread, buttered, with
   crusts removed
275ml/9½ fl oz full cream milk
50ml/2 fl oz double cream
3 eggs, slightly beaten

100g/3½ oz caster sugar
110g/4 oz sultanas
½ tsp cinnamon
grated nutmeg, whipped cream
   and fruit, to serve

Preheat the oven to 180°C/350°F/Gas Mark 4 and butter six individual dishes. Line the dishes with the buttered bread.

Add the milk and cream to the eggs and whisk, then whisk in the sugar. Add the sultanas and cinnamon to the egg mixture and pour over the bread, ensuring each slice gets its share of sultanas.

Bake for about 30 minutes or until just set.

Sprinkle with nutmeg, whipped cream and fruit of choice and serve warm.

Mark Beaumont, long-distance cyclist
born 1983

Mark Beaumont had a unique start in life, having been home-schooled until he was twelve. His parents had a sixty-acre organic smallholding long before organics and 'back to nature' became fashionable. Part of his being taught at home meant that he and his two sisters also had their own little gardens to tend, and so he was used to planting and looking after vegetables and livestock from an early age. It was a period of bucolic bliss, 'The Good Life', apart from Mark's earliest food memory: 'I remember being in my high chair and not being allowed down until I ate the dish in front of me, which I hated then and have only recently come to like – macaroni cheese. I recall having a real high-chair strop!'

His mum Una was – and still is – 'a very, very good cook. She cooked in a rustic, farmhouse style, using only seasonal food and mostly from our smallholding.' They had free-range hens and also goats which were kept mainly for the milk that they drank warm every morning or it was used to make soft cheese; sometimes they also ate goat meat. They had all sorts of vegetables (potatoes, carrots, broccoli, kale, spinach) and also an orchard with apples, pears and plums. Mark fondly remembers his mum's rustic stews and soups, but he was able to make his own rabbit stew from about the age of twelve, having killed the rabbit himself, and skinned and prepared it for the stew.

The food of Mark's childhood was very healthy. Nowadays he is a vegetarian, but he will eat wild game and seafood, since it is the industrial abattoirs, where most farmed animals are killed, with which he has a major problem. On his world tour he sometimes had to eat meat, though, as there was no alternative that would give him the daily six-thousand-calorie intake that he needed to keep cycling.

Most of his favourite childhood dishes did exclude meat: he loved his mum's vegetable stews and her wonderful cheese soufflé. 'Though that was a sort of heaven-and-hell dish as I also loathed carrot soufflé, which she often cooked. So, with my sisters, we would try to tell which it was but couldn't as both were golden-domed, until you stuck the spoon in; if it was orange we despaired as it meant it was carrot soufflé, my worst dish. I loved porridge for breakfast (we never had cooked breakfast, nor did we ever have traditional Sunday roast) and I also adored my granny's broth; proper Scotch broth, along with cauliflower soup – two of my all-time favourite soups.'

Puddings were always seasonal and so they ate apples, plums and rhubarb in abundance, often served in homely crumbles. His mum also made the most wonderful cheesecake, usually with seasonal berries in the mix.

They ate out only very seldom, such as if family were visiting, and it was always at the local Bridge of Cally Hotel. There, Mark would have the same food every time: prawn cocktail to start, any main course at all (the main did not interest him much), then cheesecake. 'I am a starter and pudding man really.'

When he took an astonishing one hundred and ninety-four days to cycle round the world, he missed certain styles of food, not necessarily particular dishes: his mum's homely touch to stews and soups, and, of course, the rustic cheesecake most of all.

Since his birthday is 1 January, Hogmanay and New Year's Day were important celebrations, with big chocolate cakes and sponge cakes featuring prominently. Una's Christmas cake was made months in advance every year and was also superb. But it was probably the thought of his mum's cheesecake that kept him going as he cycled in the remotest parts of the world for over half a year.

Fruit Cheesecake
serves 8

For the base:
175g/6 oz digestive biscuits, crushed

75g/2¾ oz butter, melted

For the filling:
280g/10 oz Philadelphia cream cheese
55g/2 oz raw brown sugar
2 tbsp honey
100g/3½ oz fruit (such as fresh or frozen
    blackcurrants, forest fruits, redcurrants,
    raspberries or blackberries)

250ml/8 fl oz double cream,
    lightly whipped
blackcurrant sprigs, to garnish

Mix together the crushed biscuits and melted butter. Press the mixture evenly into a 20cm/8 in loose-bottomed tin. Refrigerate.

Beat together the cream cheese, sugar and honey until smooth. Stir in the fruit then gently fold in the whipped cream. Spoon over the biscuit base. Refrigerate for several hours (at least 6) until firm. Remove from the tin. Decorate with blackcurrant sprigs.

Magnus Linklater, journalist and editor
born 1942

Magnus Linklater spent his first five years living on Orkney, and even when the family moved to Easter Ross in the north-east of Scotland, they still holidayed on Orkney. His abiding memory therefore is of the institution of the Orkney high tea. There was a table laden with plates of cold meat, fabulously crumbly white Orkney cheese, great bannocks (made from both beremeal and wheat flour – 'bere and floorie bannocks') and fish such as herring or trout.

Fish was another significant memory: Magnus' father used to fish in the loch near their house for trout, and they would also have seafood that is nowadays regarded as a luxury. Lobsters were eaten fairly often; Magnus' mother would come home with two huge lobsters bought at the quayside. He remembers her pushing them into massive pans of boiling water then thrusting on the lids and securing these down with two huge black irons, in case the still-very-much-alive lobsters tried to escape. The lobsters were eaten with his mother's home-made mayonnaise.

Magnus remembers that though he grew up with war-time rationing, there was always good, fresh, seasonal food, though one of his favourites was toast and dripping. When they moved to Easter Ross they had a large market garden and so there were plenty of fresh vegetables and also fruit in season. He especially remembers, as well as wonderful raspberries and strawberries, the gooseberries which his mother made into delicious gooseberry fool.

He also reminisces about raiding the kitchen when peckish: 'I remember opening a tin of condensed milk and sucking spoonfuls straight from it. There was also a strange contraption for removing the honey from the honeycomb, as my mother kept bees. But also in the pantry there would be jams – all home-made – and lots of bottled fruits. I remember sometimes the contents would ferment and so there would be a bang, and I would rush to the pantry to see plums and shattered glass everywhere!'

The nearest town when they lived in the North-East was Tain, and there they would be allowed occasional treats of fish suppers, which Magnus loved. He also adored mutton pies, drenched in grease, bought from the butcher's during a visit to town. Magnus reflects that no-one seems to eat mutton these days, but back then there was no lamb eaten, only mutton. It was rather like the chickens: only older roosters were cooked, never young birds. As for his own skills in the kitchen, he confesses, 'I am certainly no new man, but I can cook an especially good omelette.'

There was some home-baking done at home: 'I remember the large iron girdle [griddle] and my mum would make – as well as the famous Orcadian bannocks – pancakes which were a real treat for tea.'

It was possibly only at school that he came to actually hate certain foods, including lumpy porridge and milk puddings such as tapioca, sago and rice pudding. And although he now loves vegetables, back then the overcooked cabbage and spinach almost put him off for life. But he has always adored broad beans, possibly because his memories of podding them in the back garden, freshly picked from their plants, are so strong.

At New Year, the Linklater family ate roast goose, and Magnus remembers all the fat that came out of it, and then when First Footing at Hogmanay, there was always shortbread and also Black Bun. Magnus' opinion of this delicacy was similar to Robert Louis Stevenson's, which Magnus quotes to me from the famous author's 'Edinburgh Picturesque Notes': there were 'stacks of Scots Bun, a dense black substance inimical to life, and full moons of shortbread adorned with peel or sugar plum in honour of the season and the family's affections'.

But one dish Magnus remembers more fondly than Black Bun was Orkney dumplings, made for special occasions: 'They were delicious although very, very heavy. According to my Orkney cousins, it can be steamed in a cloth, like cloutie dumpling – or in a bowl. Then it was eaten hot with custard. This was a great Orkney standby and made for special high teas.'

Orkney Dumpling
serves 8

350g/12 oz self-raising flour
175g/6 oz suet
450g/1 lb mixed dried fruit
1 tsp ground cloves
1 tsp ground cinnamon
1 tsp ginger

125g/4½ oz caster sugar
1 tsp baking powder
pinch of salt
1 tbsp marmalade
2 tbsp syrup or black treacle
milk

Mix all the dry ingredients with a pinch of salt, then add the marmalade, syrup or treacle and a few drops of milk, enough to make a dropping consistency. Tip into a greased pudding bowl, cover and place in a saucepan of boiling water to steam for 4 hours. Then, in Magnus' Orcadian cousin's words, 'you have a splendid stand-by'.

Frank Hadden, Scotland rugby coach 2005–2009

born 1954

My cousin, Frank Hadden, told me his abiding memory of childhood food growing up in Dundee can be summed up in two words: fair share (or lack of it!). This meant that even if you didn't like a certain food or drink, you had it anyway. If, for example, a new packet of biscuits came into the house, it would be divided up 'mentally' between himself and his two younger brothers, David and Peter (all three boys were very close in age) and even if Frank's 'share' was three and a third, he would always push to get the fourth biscuit! When his mum, my Auntie Muriel, had made a cake, he remembers vividly fighting for the bowl and usually winning (he was biggest, after all) to eat the delicious raw cake batter.

There were many childhood dishes Frank loved, from mince, tatties and peas (tinned garden peas) to Heinz tinned treacle pudding and Fray Bentos steak and kidney pie, but it was the mention of the Dundee pie that made him most nostalgic. 'The Dundee "peh" [shortcrust pastry filled with minced beef] was a staple and served usually with beans at home. Indeed, it took a while before I acquired a taste for bridies as they were more peppery. There was also the "football peh" which was so hot and greasy, I remember one time having a blister on my chin where the boiling hot grease had run down and burned the skin.'

Another fondness he still has from childhood is for soup. When I asked him which one, he just says 'Ticky Soup' and I know exactly what he means, for my Auntie Muriel never gives a recipe, but simply says 'I just put in a wee ticky of this and a ticky of that', hence the name. Good soups they were, too!

Frank's mum used to bake cakes such as Victoria sponge, served with custard as pudding, as well as Bakewell tart, semolina or sponge pudding. Sunday breakfast was always a fry-up with everything, from tattie scones to bacon and eggs, being fried in the large frying pan. They never ate out much, although Frank can remember going out sometimes for afternoon tea and marvelling at the three-tiered cake stands groaning with sandwiches, scones and cakes. Fish suppers were an occasional treat they all loved but in Dundee the pie supper (yes, a deep-fried Scotch pie and chips!) was more popular because of the Dundonian's love of the pie. Although everyone had their favourite local chip shop, Dundee's best was, according to Frank, the Deep Sea restaurant, where you could also sit in to have fish and chips and bread and butter and a cup of tea.

'I have a big fondness for mashed potatoes, and when I was at primary school the school dinners were inedible. But if you didn't like the main course, you were allowed to have just mashed potatoes with butter, which was delicious. School rice pudding put me off the dish for years.' Another potato dish Frank loved was stovies, made in the traditional way with dripping and sometimes corned beef stirred in.

Frank also reminded me that 'Biscuits were Big' in the family, and his favourites are still custard creams and Abernethy biscuits, this latter sandwiched together with cheese and jam. Jam was also important, his mum making both raspberry and strawberry every year, although Frank admitted to me, 'Though Mum made jam, it was far runnier than shop-bought and I actually preferred shop jam as it was thicker and didn't run off your toast.'

One last testament to his sweet tooth is his fondness for ice cream, which he has always adored. There were three ice-cream shops in Dundee that they all loved, but Frank's particular favourites were the West End Café, whose ice cream was light and milky but with a strong vanilla flavour; and Robertson's the newsagents' ice cream, which was thick and creamy, not dissimilar to clotted cream ice cream nowadays. 'It was as thick as mashed potato,' he told me, 'and was heavy in the cone!' He also loved an Oyster, the wafer shells filled with ice cream (and sometimes a Snowball) and the Nougat Wafer with mallow and chocolate-coated wafers enclosing the ice cream, 'the mallow going all gooey as the ice cream melted'.

One recipe which sums up both Frank's and my own childhood memories is his mum's cloutie dumpling, which was always made for family birthdays. 'Sadly, the quality was perhaps overlooked by the chance of finding the silver threepenny (replaced later by a sixpence) wrapped in greaseproof paper inside the dumpling,' he told me. Just like the cake bowl and the biscuit packet, there was some fighting going on – for the coin – but this time the fight was not with his two brothers but with the dumpling itself!

Muriel Hadden's Cloutie Dumpling
serves 8

Sue says: The word cloth is the origin of this dumpling recipe, as 'cloot' or 'clout' is Scots for cloth, and it refers to the cloth in which the dumpling is boiled. Unlike any other dumplings or steamed puddings, it forms a characteristic 'skin', made by sprinkling flour and sugar into the cloth before filling with the mixture.

The skin must be dried off before serving – done nowadays in the oven, although it used to be done in front of the open fireplace. It was made only for special occasions such as birthdays (in which case there were silver threepennies hidden inside, similar to charms in a Christmas pudding). It would then be eaten with custard. Next day, any leftovers would be served for breakfast: sliced and fried in rendered suet and eaten with bacon.

If you want to add coins, wrap five-pence pieces or charms in waxed or greaseproof paper and add to the mixture. This is my Auntie Muriel's recipe, one of our family's treasures.

225g/8 oz plain flour, sifted
200g/7 oz golden caster sugar
1 level tsp ground cinnamon
1 heaped tsp mixed spice
110g/4 oz shredded suet
110g/4 oz sultanas

110g/4 oz currants
110g/4 oz stoned dates, finely chopped
1 heaped tsp bicarbonate of soda
approx. 200ml/7 fl oz milk, sour milk or
    cold tea
flour and caster sugar, to sprinkle

Mix the first 9 ingredients together in a bowl with enough liquid to make a soft dough of a stiff, dropping consistency.

Dip a large pudding cloth (or tea towel) into boiling water then drain well and lay out flat on a table. Sprinkle with flour and then sugar (I use my flour and sugar shakers): you want an even – but not thick – sprinkling. Place the mixture in the middle of the cloth then tie up the cloth securely with string, allowing a little room for expansion. Place on a heatproof plate in the bottom of a large saucepan. Top up with boiling water to just cover the pudding then cover with a lid and simmer gently for 3¾–4 hours. Check the water level occasionally and top up if necessary. (You should continually hear the reassuring, gentle shuddering sound of the plate on the bottom of the pan for the entire duration of cooking.)

Wearing oven gloves, remove the pudding from the pan, dip briefly into a bowl of cold water: for no more than 10 seconds – so the skin does not stick to the cloth. Cut the string, untie the cloth and invert the dumpling onto an ovenproof plate. Place in an oven preheated to 180°C/350°F/Gas 4 for 10–15 minutes – just until the skin feels less sticky – then sprinkle with caster sugar and serve hot with custard *and* ice cream!

Rory Bremner, comedian
and political satirist
born 1961

Growing up in Edinburgh, some of Rory Bremner's earliest memories of food were his mum's fish pie, enhanced with curry powder and hard-boiled eggs. She also made good rissoles, wholesome soups, mince and tatties and sometimes served up a Macsween haggis for a treat. Her trifle was legendary, but fairly traditional, made with tinned mandarin oranges and custard.

Two vivid memories of eating outside the home are of Lucas ice cream in Musselburgh (just outside Edinburgh), where they would pop in on the way home from a day at Gullane beach; Rory loved the strawberry flavoured ice cream. Also, when they went to St Andrews for the Lammas Fair, he would be bought a bridie from Fisher & Donaldson, the famous baker, which he loved. Later on he remembers excellent fish and chips from The International Fish Bar in Edinburgh: 'It was here I first witnessed a pizza being deep-fried. Unbelievable!'

School food was easily forgettable, it was all rather bland. 'At twelve o'clock every day one of the dinner ladies would pass the window of our classroom and we would ask her what was for lunch. Every single day, she'd reply, "Soop, meat an' puddin'!"'

The Bremner family would occasionally eat out as a treat. There was a restaurant on North Bridge called Darling's that served braised beef with mashed potatoes shaped with an ice cream scoop. 'Dad stood at the bar just drinking, refusing to eat a thing there, funnily enough!'

Rory remembers tablet (which he still adores), kippers from Millers the fishmonger's near the King's Theatre and, of course, porridge, which was simply part of everyday growing up. One unusual memory was frozen cubes of Irn-Bru, which he would remove from the ice tray and suck. 'It was the excitement of having a brand new freezer; we froze everything we could. Later on, as a teenager, I was into wine-making and froze cubes of white wine. Dad thought it was tonic water and added it to his gin. He wasn't very happy!'

Picnics were always fun as a child and Rory remembers the best picnic fare was – and still is for him – a Scottish floury bap thickly spread with butter, filled with salad and plenty of sliced ham. Continuing the cold meat theme, he told me about the family's favourite lunch: 'We called it "The Investiture Lunch" as the first we had was in 1969 when Prince Charles was invested at Caernarvon Castle. Mum bought lots of different salamis, hams and cheese from Victor Hugo's, the wonderful Edinburgh delicatessen (I used to love the smells in there), and these were all laid out on the table and we would have that with some French bread. We all loved Investiture Lunches!

'I also adored – as did my dad – the chocolate cake in The Laigh Bake House in Hanover Street. It was run by a very "Edinburgh Lady" called Joan Spicer and I will never forget going in there after John Smith's funeral and saying to her how sad it was. She replied, in her refined Morningside accent, "Yes, I know, but didn't we do the funeral well!"'

Though he loves cooking at home these day (marinated tuna, wild mushroom risotto, salmon fillet with pesto crust being some of his favourite dishes), he still becomes all misty-eyed when talking about Scotland's fine ingredients – strawberries, raspberries, shellfish and venison: some of the best.

Nigel Slater's Lemon Trifle
serves 6

Though Mum's trifle was wonderful, Nigel Slater's is delicious, but it is so rich we call it 'Death by Trifle' in my family. Thanks to Nigel, this is taken from *The Kitchen Diaries*.

100g sponge fingers
100g lemon or orange curd
3 tbsp limoncello

500ml double cream
120g caster sugar
100ml lemon juice

To finish:
250ml whipping or double cream
1 small orange

crystallised violets

Break the sponge fingers in half then spread thickly with the curd. Put them in a glass or china dish and sprinkle over the limoncello. Pour the 500ml cream into a saucepan and add the sugar. Bring to the boil over a moderate heat then turn down the heat and leave to simmer for a good 2–3 minutes. Remove from the heat and stir in the lemon juice, then pour this mixture over the sponge fingers. They may bob about a bit in the lemon custard but just push them down and leave to cool. When the mixture has cooled, refrigerate for a couple of hours, or even overnight, until set.

To finish, whip the 250ml cream until thick, but stop before it stands in peaks. It should still be able to slide slowly from a spoon. Smooth the cream loosely over the trifle then finely grate the orange zest over the top and add a few violets. Return briefly to the fridge until needed.

Jackie Kay, poet and novelist
born 1961

It was the 'complete unpredictability of a bowl of porridge' that Jackie Kay remembers as a child, growing up in Bishopbriggs near Glasgow. 'It could be lumpy, too salty, was always grey and to me was associated with depression. It was eaten a lot at home and I hated it – still do!'

But she also had good memories: the family used to holiday on the Isle of Mull and they all fell in love with Mull Cheddar. They used to eat big chunks of it, as if it were big blocks of tablet. 'But as well as associating Mull with the lovely cheese, I also remember when I was about four years old, stepping off the boat in Tobermory and some of the locals asking my parents, "Do they have the English?" as my brother and I were obviously the only non-white children they had seen!'

Jackie remembers her Auntie Peggy making her a boiled egg and hating that as it was far too runny, but, as was the habit in those days, she was forced to eat it. She did, however, like 'Champed Egg': warm, hard-boiled egg mashed up in a cup with butter and salt. And she adored her granny's soup, made from a hough bone, the meat then shredded into the soup with perfectly diced carrots, diced potatoes, barley, marrowfat peas and red lentils. 'Granny made this on Wednesdays and my dad would visit her then and bring home the pot of soup for us. Then when we all visited her on Sunday, we would return the empty pot to her.'

Neither her mum nor dad were great cooks, but her mum's macaroni cheese was delicious: boiled Marshalls' macaroni layered up with slices of tomato, grated cheese, chopped bacon and onions all over, then oven-baked until golden and gooey. Indeed, Jackie still makes a version these days, albeit rather more elaborate.

Her parents were both members of the Communist Party and with that, according to Jackie, came many perks: on Saturdays her dad would go to the Party butcher and be given four steaks and four slices of square (beef) sausage for free. If anyone in the Party needed a carpenter or plumber, it would also be easily arranged. When her parents went to Russia to be with fellow Communists, Jackie and her brother were left with family friends, apart from a couple of days when they stayed near Edinburgh. 'I will never forget the gooseberry pie made by the little old man we were left with. This was a pie out of a fairytale, just divine. It was really juicy and thick and the flavours all burst in the mouth. There was a hole in the middle of it and the syrupy gooseberries oozed out. The old man had a long overgrown path he had to go down to pick the gooseberries from the garden of his wee cottage. I will never forget that pie.'

And on the pastry theme, just as Jackie associates gooseberry pie with overgrown gardens, she associates apple pie with bright little birds: her Aunt Agnes taught Jackie to make shortcrust pastry and, once it was made, they would go out to her uncle's aviary in the garden shed, where she would look at the beautiful and brightly coloured birds. Her aunt's apple tarts, made from the freshly made pastry, were memorable.

Jackie learned to do some basic cooking at home but the thing she loved doing most was 'making a plate'. Her mum would sometimes say, 'Let's make a plate to cheer ourselves up'. On this plate were beetroot balls, slices of ham, cubes of cheese, pickled onions 'and a happy yellow pineapple ring' (as written in her poem *Yellow*). She still remembers the strong complementary colours all beautifully laid out for them to enjoy. She also learned to poach smoked haddock in milk and make omelettes.

Whereas in the majority of Scottish homes Christmas or Hogmanay were the most important occasions, in the Communist household in which Jackie grew up, it was Burns Night, since 'Burns is very much celebrated by Communists. Going to Burns Suppers made me realise I too wanted to be a poet. It was the theatre of it all, listening to the *Ode to the Haggis* recited with such drama. My dad often recited *The Immortal Memory* and we went – sometimes twice a month – to Burns Suppers, from when I was quite tiny. I loved eating haggis (now, I don't eat meat but enjoy vegetarian haggis) and love the colours of the orange neeps, creamy white tatties and brown-flecked haggis. I also love the fun and relaxation of eating at a long table with lots of people.'

These days Jackie still likes to cook haggis and also broth and smoked fish. But two of her mum's dishes she loved then and now are rice pudding (which Jackie liked to see emerge from the oven topped with crusty skin, though she never liked to eat it) and apple sponge pudding, made in a square tin.

Never-fail Apple Sponge
serves 6

Here's my mum's recipe for her apple sponge, which she got from a little cookery book when she lived in New Zealand, printed by Christchurch West High School.

1.3kg/3 lb cooking apples

2 tbsp sugar

For the sponge:

2 very large eggs (or 3 medium-sized ones)

½ tsp bicarbonate of soda

125g/4½ oz caster sugar

125g/4½ oz plain flour

1 tsp cream of tartar

Peel and core the apples and slice them very thinly, laying them in the bottom of a 23cm/9 in square baking tin. Sprinkle with sugar.

For the sponge, beat the eggs and soda together well. Add the sugar very slowly and beat it in thoroughly (several minutes in a food mixer). Sift in the flour with the cream of tartar and fold in gently.

Pour this mixture over the apples. Put the tin in an oven preheated to 180°C/350°F/Gas 4 for 15–20 minutes until just set.

Sue says: I prefer to cook the apples first in a microwave bowl for a few minutes until just done, then drain off any excess liquid before laying them over the base of the tin.

Brian Cox, actor
born 1946

'Probably my earliest childhood food memory would be, I suppose, fish and chips from Del Nevo's Fish and Chip shop in Victoria Street, Dundee. Also Abernethy Ice-cream shop in the same street, where I would always get the vanilla flavour.'

Brian Cox recalls home-cooking growing up in Dundee: 'My mother was a good baker. Meat was all right if it was stewed. Meat that had to be prepared delicately I think she simply didn't have the skill or understanding back then. Things I remember her making that were delicious were baked rice made in an ashet dish – I loved the skin on it. Food was more functional than important in our household, in a way. I think in a lot of Scottish households, especially working class ones at that time, it was just more functional. One of the best things my mum made was soups, though – like a kale soup and a ham rib broth, sometimes a lentil and split pea broth.'

And when asked about any childhood dishes he now craves when he is abroad, he told me of his love of Forfar bridies. 'I used to go to Wallace's, the old Dundee pie shop, and have a great tea of bridies, HP Sauce and baked beans. I occasionally still crave them because they were tasty and comforting. In the early days I would buy some bridies and put them out on the radiator of my car as I was driving down to Jedburgh [in the Scottish Borders] to keep them hot!'

There was very little eating out when Brian was a child, but he told me the family were mainly always at the chipper. After Del Nevo's closed because poor Giuseppe (Joe) died, they went to Espositos on Albert Street. He always loved fish suppers – made of course with haddock – but he also confessed to a love of pudding suppers too: 'I like black pudding, though I only developed a taste for white pudding later in life.'

He absolutely hated school dinners: 'They were shocking. There was this thing they used to have called mince which wasn't mince at all – it was like an oatmeal porridge or something which was made to look like mince and it was disgusting.'

He never learned to cook or bake at home really, but he picked it up late, remembering what his mother used to do and would give it a try. One of the earliest dishes he did learn to make was French toast: 'Because sometimes my mother would forget to feed me, I used to make the French toast for my dinner. I was about ten when I started, I think. The trick I eventually found was to let it steep in the egg and milk mixture until it almost falls apart, and then you quickly fry it.'

He seldom makes Scottish dishes now, although he sometimes eats haggis – the taste for which he acquired later in life. And when he does return to Scotland, he loves to eat really good fish and chips and also haggis and neeps. He tells me there is a really good fish and chip shop in Arbroath, just north of Dundee now.

Brian also remembers how special New Year was in Dundee: 'I remember my mother used to cook all night on Hogmanay – she would be in her dressing gown at 4am cooking. She would make big stews and also oven-baked stews. I remember at Christmas time the luxury was a chicken. We had roast chicken on Christmas Day.'

Dundee Apple Tart
serves 6

Sue says: One of Brian's fond memories is of the very shallow apple tart his mum used to make all the time which is – hopefully – just like my recipe here, developed for him.

4 cooking apples, peeled, sliced thinly
2 tbsp sugar (or 1 tbsp 'agave nectar'
    for diabetics, as Brian is now)
½ tsp cinnamon

juice of 1 lemon
350g/12 oz shortcrust pastry
milk and sugar, to glaze

Place the apples in a microwave bowl with the sugar (or agave), cinnamon and lemon juice. Cover tightly and cook for about 5 minutes until softened but still a little firm. Drain over a sieve and cool.

Roll out the pastry to fit a shallow tart tin (approx 23cm/9 in), fill with the apples then roll out another piece of pastry to cover. Seal the edges, then paint the surface with some milk. Sprinkle with a little sugar (but not if cooking for diabetics). Slash 2 holes in the top for the steam to escape then bake in an oven preheated to 190°C/375°F/Gas 5 for 35–40 minutes or until the pastry is golden.

Gordon Brown, Prime Minister
born 1951

'Growing up in Kirkcaldy, my father was the minister of our local church. This meant that our home, the manse, was always open to visitors. People would call in to speak to my mum and dad about all kinds of local activities to get their support and involvement, or just to have a chat. Everyone was always invited for a cup of tea and sometimes to eat. My mum would always have a huge pot of soup sitting on the stove so there was always something hot and nourishing to offer guests. As one of three boys we had great appetites, so she was also busy making big stews or Sunday roasts served with potatoes and vegetables. I never had a problem eating my greens, and my favourites are probably sprouts because I associate them with my mum's great Christmas roasts. We lived by the sea so we grew up eating lots of fish as well.'

They hardly ever had sweets, but there was always a pudding with their supper and, he says, 'I've never quite given up that habit!' In the summertime, they would go out picking raspberries and would have those with ice cream as a treat. 'My mum was also a great apple crumble and custard person, which we all loved. My dad had to look after the cooking for a long time once while my mother was unwell. He had only one dish that he made: omelettes with cornflour – an ingredient I have never understood for an omelette to this day! But I do remember how hard he tried to make sure that my brothers and I were well fed and looked after in my mother's absence. I'm not much better at cooking myself but I'm OK at rustling up a simple lunch or supper for the boys when needs be, and the microwave is a wonderful invention for when I'm on my own or working late. My father could have done with one of those!'

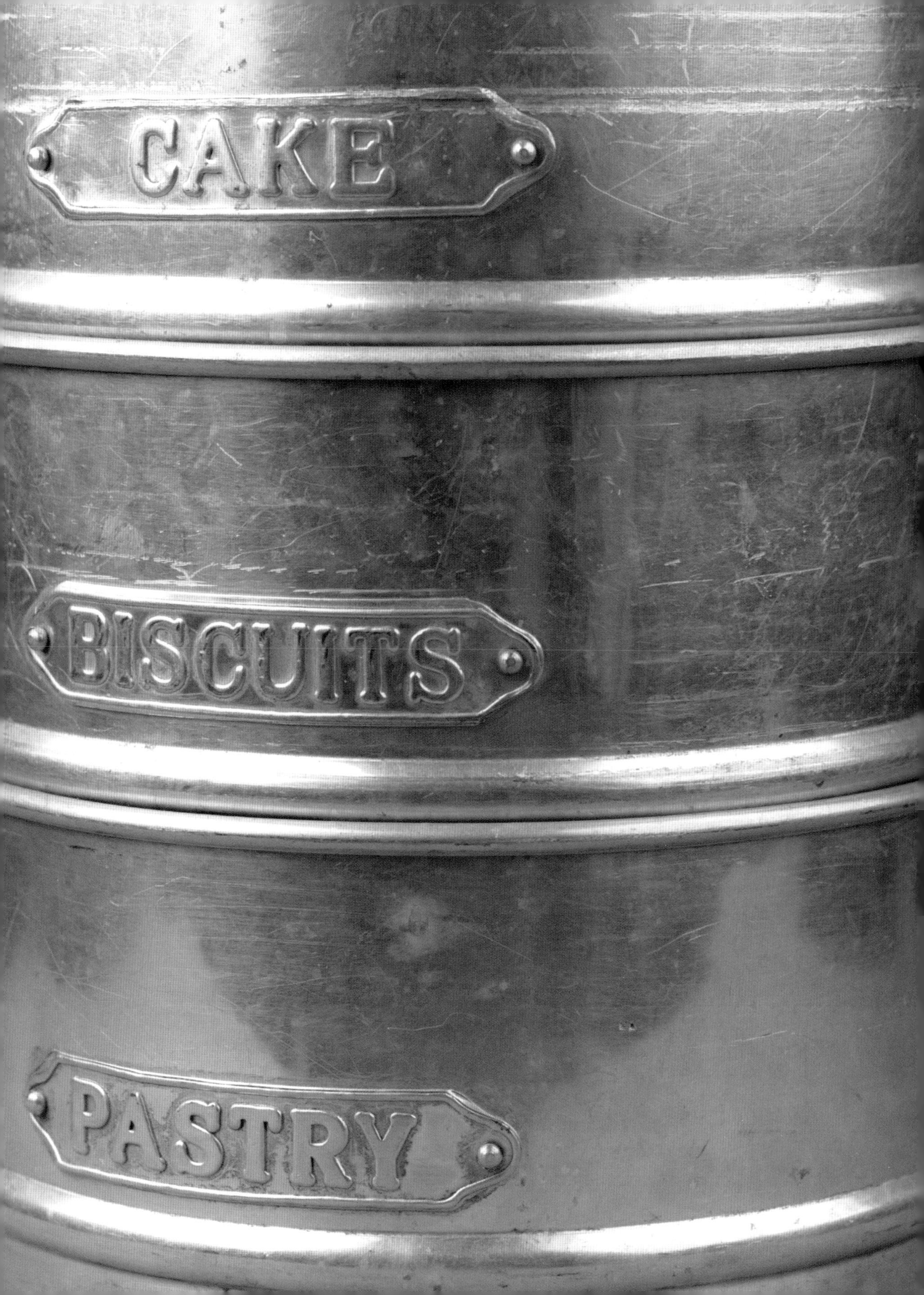
CAKE
BISCUITS
PASTRY

Apple and Blackberry Crumble

serves 4

175g/6 oz flour (a mixture of brown and
    white flour is best)
50g/1¾ oz low-fat margarine
50g/1¾ oz butter
50g/1¾ oz soft brown sugar, plus an
    extra 3 tbsp

2 tbsp muesli (optional)
225g/8 oz cooking apples, peeled,
    cored and cut into chunks
225g/8 oz blackberries (or rhubarb
    washed and cut into small chunks,
    or raspberries in the summer)

Preheat the oven to 200°C/400°F/Gas 6.

Put the flour, margarine and butter into a big mixing bowl and rub together through
your fingers until it looks like breadcrumbs. Stir in the 50g/1¾ oz sugar, and for a little
extra crunch, add a handful of muesli, if you like.

Load the apple chunks and blackberries (or other fruit) into a pie dish. Sprinkle 3
tablespoons of sugar over the fruit and a tiny dash of water. Pile the crumble mixture
over the fruit, smoothing over to make a flat surface without pressing down too hard.

Bake in the oven for about 25 minutes until the crumble top is golden and you can
just see the fruit bubbling at the edges.

You can serve the crumble straightaway with custard, yoghurt or ice cream, but it is
also good cold if you have any left over the next day.

Sue says: I add an extra 50g/1¾ oz butter to the crumble to make it moist.

bakes

John Barrowman, actor
and musical performer
born 1967

'Oh, I have lots of early food memories,' says John Barrowman about his Glasgow childhood. 'The Barrowmans love their food, especially desserts. I remember a family wedding where everyone, including the bridal party, was already seated to be served dinner and we were still checking out the dessert buffet. You've got to plan your main course around the dessert options. Everyone knows that. Probably my earliest memory, though, is of my Gran Butler – her name was Marion but we called her Murn – making me chips and deep frying Spam slices in her Sandyhills flat. She had the mankiest pot of lard in her cupboard that she recycled for everything fried, so no matter what she made, it tasted really delicious and always had a hint of the flavours of the last foods cooked in the pan. Yum!'

John's mum is a good baker and his other gran, Emily Barrowman, used to make 'the most amazing pancakes; and my sister, Carole, has inherited that skill. In the States we eat them for breakfast and top them with butter, syrup or fresh fruit. When I was a boy, at my Gran Barrowman's on a Sunday she'd make pancakes for lunch and we'd layer them with her home-made jams. Now that I think about it, both my mum and my Gran Barrowman made lots of home-made jams – gooseberry was a family favourite.'

John's mum, also named Marion, would make him a soft-boiled egg with toast cut into thin 'soldiers' for his tea when he was a child, and John told me he still makes a 'boiled egg with soldiers' when he is by himself. He also loves a big American breakfast: waffles or pancakes, eggs, toast, sausages, crunchy bacon and hash browns, which he insists must be crispy round the edges. When he was growing up in America (the family moved to the States in 1976 when he was eight), his mum often cooked a big breakfast on a Saturday morning and he'd stay in bed until he couldn't resist the smells wafting up the stairs.

'When we lived in Scotland, I have memories of eating at friends' and family members' houses pretty regularly, and on Sundays we'd eat a formal lunch at my Gran Barrowman's house. We were usually joined by my cousins and so the food memories are mixed up with memories of playing with them. When we moved to the States, my mum, dad and I and some good friends, who had three girls around my age, would have "Dallas Nights" on Friday nights.

We'd all go out to the Moose Lodge for dinner, usually a cod or perch fish fry, and then we'd come back to our house to eat sweets and watch *Dallas*. That was heaven!'

When I asked John about his preference for a fish or pudding supper from the chip shop, he told me enigmatically, 'I'm a bit like Captain Jack in this regard. I can go either way – fish supper or black pudding!'

He hated tripe as a child: 'No question about it. My mum would stretch the food budget when we were very young and one night a week she'd make tripe with a side of mashed potatoes so we'd have something to soak up the oniony-milky broth the tripe floated in – yes, we would have to finish the broth because 'all the goodness is in the broth. On those nights, we could eat in front of the TV– as if that would make it taste better.'

John grew up around a number of very capable women: 'my mum, Murn, and Murn's sister, Jeannie – and each one could cook. In fact, when I was growing up the kitchen was always the heart of the house. As a result, I love to cook and I'm pretty good at it. When I have time, I do most of the cooking. Fresh salmon is fantastic. Actually, I like to experiment with different ways to cook and dress fish. Of course, I must admit I also love all the things that go along with the art of cooking – the gadgets, the dishes, the utensils, the big shiny pots and pans!'

And as for cooking Scottish dishes, John's niece, Clare, and he have assisted his mum in making cloutie dumpling, a staple for the family's Christmas dinner. 'My mum puts healthy amounts of whisky and brandy in her recipe. I think Clare and I both still need some practice. This is a family food tradition I don't want to lose. There's nothing better after a delicious Christmas dinner than a thick slice of cloutie dumpling swimming in condensed milk or covered in fresh cream. After my mum has wrapped the mixture in the clout, and before she immerses it in the pot of boiling water, everyone in the kitchen has to "slap the dumpling's bum" so it develops a good thick skin. Works every time.'

When he returns to Scotland, John likes to order a fish supper and he always has to buy a supply of Irn-Bru to have on hand for family when they visit him in London or Cardiff.

Recalling special family occasions, he told me about the importance of Hogmanay and New Year's Day, even now. 'At Hogmanay my mum bakes shortbread and we have to greet the New Year with that and slices of Black Bun. Oh, and wee drams of whisky for my dad and not-so-wee glasses of champagne for the rest of us. New Year's Day we have my mum's steak pie with a flaky crust, roast potatoes and Brussels sprouts. Dessert is usually trifle and mince pies. My mouth is watering.'

Banana and Honey Bread

makes one loaf

This is my mum Marion's recipe.

225g/8 oz plain flour
1 tsp baking powder
pinch of salt
115g/4 oz butter, diced
85g/3 oz light brown sugar

200g/7 oz raisins
3 medium-sized ripe bananas
2 tbsp clear/runny honey
2 eggs

Sift together the flour, baking powder and a pinch of salt. Rub in the butter until it resembles breadcrumbs. Stir in the sugar and raisins. Mash the bananas in a separate bowl.

Whisk together the honey and eggs then add this to the dry ingredients, combining well. Pour into a buttered, base-lined loaf tin (900g/2 lb) and bake for 80–90 minutes, covering loosely with foil for the last 30 minutes. Cook until a skewer comes out clean.

Cool in the tin for 5 minutes then remove carefully to a wire rack to cool completely before cutting.

Sue says: This is also delicious served slightly warm as a pudding with honeycomb ice cream and strawberries.

Kevin MacNeil, author
born 1972

Kevin MacNeil's earliest food memory from his childhood in Stornoway, on the Isle of Lewis, was of sitting in the back garden chewing on some coal! 'There is a photo in which I look literally, but not metaphorically, black-affronted,' he told me.

There was also, of course, proper food: 'My mum and every granny-type character on the street was a great cook/baker. MacLeod Road in Stornoway and the other streets around it were genuinely neighbourly in those days. There was a real feeling of community. I used to cut the grass for some of the elderly neighbours and they would always "repay" me in home-made scones, plum duff, and so on.'

Since Kevin has been a fish-eating vegetarian for more than a decade, there are very few of the meals he ate as a child that he now craves, since 'many of the best-known Lewis dishes are distinctly un-vegetarian: *marag dhubh* [Gaelic for the famous Stornoway black pudding], guga [gannet], Lewis lamb, and so on. We used to have steak and chips on a late Saturday afternoon and I remember enjoying mince, fish fingers and salmon (best when poached by a friend). Then there was Angel Delight, Swiss Roll – and the coming of the microwave meant we ate more ready meals, such as chicken korma curry, that tasted like plastic. Nowadays, although I no longer eat meat, I reckon my diet is more varied and more healthy. I don't remember eating exotic foods like pasta very often, and my taste buds simply weren't very well travelled until I was an adult. My favourite childhood dish was, sadly and Scottishly enough, fish and chips. I've lived abroad for spells of my adult life and that was the one meal I would really yearn for while living outside Scotland.'

He ate out only seldom when he was growing up. In those days, eating out meant a bar lunch and, according to Kevin, your options were limited. He is pleased to see that nowadays Stornoway is much more cosmopolitan, even having a critically lauded Thai restaurant.

But his childhood favourite at the chip shop was 'Cheeky Chips! I mentioned these in both my novel *The Stornoway Way* and song "Local Man Ruins Everything", so they must have had some unconscious influence on me. On a Saturday or some other day off school you would treat yourself after swimming/cycling/playing football/messing about in the castle grounds to

a well-earned portion of Cheeky Chips. This was a little bucket of chips with a battered sausage, for about thirty pence. Drowning in grease and vinegar and oh so delicious to our hungry young mouths.'

There was only one thing he hated as a child and that was mushrooms. 'They are evil – the very spawn of Satan. Don't get me started on mushrooms. I shudder at the word and all my friends know not to mention them in my presence!'

Kevin's mum encouraged his brother and him to become quite independent at a young age, so they learned to do lots of domestic tasks like ironing and baking: his brother's speciality was bran loaf and Kevin's was banana loaf.

Now living in Shetland, he tends to eat quite a lot of fish so he likes to buy local fish and other produce as much as he can. His cooking does not have a particularly Scottish flavour, though, as he eats a lot of pasta, rice and lentils and loves Italian food and spicy curries. 'And one of the best meals of my life was the porridge our Zen cook made at a Zen retreat in Wales some years ago; it was loaded with nuts, fruits and other random goodies. I have improvised my own version incorporating cinnamon and honey and a variety of nuts and fruits. It's a wonderful start to a winter's day.'

Banana Loaf
makes 1 loaf

225g/8 oz self-raising flour
150g/5½ oz sugar
pinch of salt

1 large egg
3 ripe bananas, mashed
55g/2 oz butter

Mix together the flour, sugar and salt. Whip the egg and add it to the mashed bananas. Melt the butter and mix everything together. Place in a well-greased 900g/2 lb loaf tin and bake for 1 hour in an oven preheated to 190°C/375°F/Gas 5.

Leave in the tin to cool for half an hour or so before turning out.

Andrew Marr, broadcaster
born 1959

'I am ashamed to say my first memory of eating anything was a Milky Bar!' Andrew chuckles. But he also recalls eating oatcakes from an early age; he was allowed one spread with marmalade, but only after eating two pieces of toast!

Food was very important in the Marr family and Andrew's mum learned a lot about cooking from a lady in the village, Mrs Scott – traditional recipes such as marmalade, jam and scones. They stayed in Longforgan, in the Carse of Gowrie between Dundee and Perth. And since this is one of the best berry areas in the country, Andrew also recalls 'going to the berries' as a child to earn money. Just as I used to do, he would strap his luggie (bucket) to his waist then pick all along the length of the dreel (row) of tall raspberry canes before finally getting them weighed at the end. Andrew said he earned a lot of money picking berries (I did not, as I ate most of mine!). Even now he remembers the fabulous smell of jam pervading the entire house when his mum was doing a big boiling of raspberry jam in the kitchen.

He also remembers butteries from his childhood and lots of fish, bought from the fish van. He was always a huge fan of Arbroath Smokies. He also told me about going fishing in the lochs of the West Highlands and catching brown trout. These would be coated in oatmeal and fried in butter, sometimes served with bacon. His mum was also great at stews and casseroles and made excellent raised game or pork pies. He loved soup, his favourite being a thick mushroom soup, but his dad's broth, all bulging with pearl barley and flavoured with mutton bones, was also superb.

When I asked him if the family ever ate out he told me about family outings to a milk bar – the same one I went to with my Granny Anderson for fresh cream cakes. 'Because Mum was a strict church-goer, she never cooked on a Sunday and so we would often go to the Horn Milk Bar where we had such exotica as gammon, pineapple and chips! There was another milk bar (all very 1960s) in Fife when we visited my other grandparents – and I remember the wonderful taste of real milkshakes. As a teenager I used to love fish suppers and I also reckon a white pudding supper is a very fine thing.'

Andrew learned to cook the basics at home before university – white sauce, basic casseroles and stews. At school, he loathed macaroni cheese and also the stringy grey dish that they called stew. 'However, unusually, I adored tapioca pudding with jam; but I was a very greedy boy!'

Another dish Andrew becomes thoroughly nostalgic about is a good mutton pie (the Scotch pie is very popular in the Dundee area). He liked them warm or cold, bought from a good butcher and eaten with plenty of Worcestershire sauce sloshed down the hole in the middle. He also loved a good Forfar bridie, preferably with home-made mango chutney.

Nowadays he loves to cook dishes such as casseroles, fish pie and kedgeree, from his childhood. 'But I'd say most cooking I do now has more spice and also is a lot lighter. My Scottishness is evident very much in my addiction to salty butter, anything with oats (porridge in winter, muesli in summer) and I am a devoted whisky man!'

He also remembered tablet and fudge, cakes and sweeties and plenty of stewed rhubarb – as they grew rhubarb in the garden, along with potatoes and carrots. A bramble and apple pie with custard was another great favourite, made from wild brambles growing all round the country lanes nearby.

Whenever he returns to Scotland now, his pie obsession re-emerges: 'I always seek out decent mutton pies and those little rhubarb pies, glazed on top, from a good baker.' When I reminded him about the famous Dundee baker Fisher & Donaldson and their rhubarb pies, he concurred theirs were the best, as were the amazing chocolate violets from Goodfellow & Steven, another Dundee baker. The memory of his first ever Lees macaroon bar (another favourite) is charming: his uncle had an open-top sports car and he took young Andrew out for a drive, armed with said macaroon bar. 'This was a memory you don't forget.'

Hogmanay was very important: 'We always went over the road and the great treat was good Black Bun, all spicy, cut thinly and eaten with slices of "gum-ripping" Cheddar cheese. This was, of course, accompanied by whisky. Christmas was another traditional feast, with Christmas pudding being the highlight. I used to love it so much there was at least one occasion my dad gave me bicarbonate of soda and sent me into the garden to be sick, I had eaten so much pudding and had become decidedly green!'

Sticky Gingerbread
makes 1 loaf

This is my Aunt Sheila's recipe; profoundly corrupt and sybaritic people will whack a dod of salty butter onto slices of this gingerbread.

225g/8 oz butter
225g/8 oz soft dark brown sugar
280g/10 oz black treacle
280g/10 oz plain flour
2 tsp ground ginger

1 tsp ground cinnamon
2 large eggs
1 tsp bicarbonate of soda
100ml/3½ fl oz/½ cup milk, warmed

Heat the first 3 ingredients in a pan until liquid.

Meanwhile, sift the flour, ginger and cinnamon into a big bowl. Beat in the eggs. Dissolve the bicarbonate of soda in the warm milk and add this to the mixture. Mix everything together and put it into one or two lined loaf tins.

Cook for 50 minutes–one hour in an oven preheated to 180°C/350°F/Gas 4 (less in a fan oven, obviously), but the only way to reckon it is ready is by the smell! It should sink, with an air of gentle resignation, in the centre, producing a moist effect which is entirely delectable.

LYLE'S BLAC

ABRAM LYLE

OUT OF THE STRONG CAME F

SUGAR RE

454g

Siobhan Redmond, actor
born 1959

Siobhan Redmond's first memory associated with food is of walking around with an apple on a ribbon round her neck. The ribbon went right through the core and she was given this so she could continue to nibble on it and not drop it. She also remembers eating slices of raw turnip with (if her Auntie Nessie was around) a big glass of American Cream Soda.

Food was important in Siobhan's home, growing up in Glasgow in the 1960s. Unusually, her father did much of the cooking: 'Which was good, apart from all the offal-y things he liked. But what I liked were the stories that came with the food: so a fish cake would come with the tale of fish swimming from Norway with a fish cake on its head!' She did not like tripe or boiled tongue and, again perhaps unusually, was not forced to eat it; her father would allow her and her sister to try something twice and then if they still did not like it, he would not offer them it again. He was a good, plain cook, although loved to try 'adventurous' things such as snails or consommé. 'What he did not like to cook, though, was Bappery – all the scones and cakes and teabreads.'

So although her father avoided Bappery, Siobhan's aunts did plenty of home-baking. Her Auntie Nessie's scones were wonderful; indeed she says she still longs for a treacle scone like her auntie used to make.

Her favourites – then and now – were kedgeree, herring in oatmeal, and kippers. 'And I did, of course, like the occasional bout of Bappery myself! And as for tablet, though I loved it, my teeth ache now at the very mention of it.'

The family did sometimes eat out, often in Strathavon in a hotel for high tea, where she remembers 'a meringue as big as your head!' She realises now some of the purpose of these high-tea outings (though they also went to Chinese and Italian restaurants) was that her parents wanted the family to be able to conduct themselves well in public. Fish and chips were also sometimes permitted and her favourite was Mister Bonacorsi in Glasgow's Tollcross, where she always had fish cooked in breadcrumbs, not batter. She still loves good fish and chips but always prefers the crumbed fish.

As well as offal, Siobhan hated butter beans with a vengeance and – the few times they ate them – tinned mixed vegetables. There was also her Auntie Mary's mince custard; basically mince cooked underneath a savoury egg custard. And although her sister once said she refused to eat porridge as it was 'bear's food', Siobhan loves eating it – but only ever with salt and water, never milk or cream and sugar.

She seldom cooks now, preferring to eat the ingredients raw. 'My father was quite pleased his daughters couldn't cook as they would then have to find men to cook for them – or earn enough themselves to eat out!'

When she returns to Scotland, she loves eating her childhood favourites and seeks out a fruit scone – but never served hot. 'We Scots know the butter should never melt on a scone!' And another of her all-time favourites was a coffee bun, which her 'Auntie Cathie Murray' (not a real aunt) used to make.

Coffee Buns
makes 12

Sue says: Siobhan's sister could not find her old recipe so I tried various ones to come up with the description of both texture and appearance given by Siobhan. Some recipes use soft brown sugar but these, below, are more the right texture which has a hint of a rock bun but not as hard, and also of an American cookie but not as crisp. The presence of coffee in the recipe is mainly for colour so don't worry if you can't taste it. Milk can be used instead of egg to glaze, though egg is traditional as it makes the top glossier. My recipe will hopefully meet with Siobhan's approval.

150g/5½ oz butter, softened
150g/5½ oz unrefined Demerara sugar
1 large egg
15ml (1 tbsp) coffee essence (or 1 tbsp
   strong black coffee, cooled)

300g/10 oz self-raising flour, sifted
50g/1¾ oz currants
a pinch of salt
1 beaten egg yolk, to glaze

Cream the butter and sugar together. Beat in the egg then the coffee essence. Add in the flour, currants and a pinch of salt then, using your hands, roll into 12 balls.

Place on a greased baking sheet and flatten slightly. Brush the top with the egg yolk then bake in an oven preheated to 190°C/375°F/Gas 5 for about 15 minutes or until golden and just firm.

Remove to a wire rack to cool.

Catherine Lockerbie, Director, Edinburgh International Book Festival
born 1958

Catherine Lockerbie can vividly recall two food-related childhood memories: the first is of a slice of white bread, spread with margarine and sprinkled with white sugar. The second is of soft-boiled eggs and toast soldiers when she was ill in bed. 'I was a very sickly child, having had hepatitis which kept me off primary school a lot, and so I remember the boiled eggs; and to drink, Lucozade, which I now loathe.'

Food wasn't hugely important as she grew up, but they did have good wholesome meals every day: 'There was an awful lot of "meat with carbohydrate".' Every day when they came home from school for lunch she and her brother would have a three-course meal – soup (often broth with a ham bone), stew or sausages, then a dessert such as rice pudding or bread and butter pudding. When they lived in Aberdeen, in the evening the four of them had high tea, but when, in 1967, they moved to Bridge of Allan, Catherine's great-aunt lived with them, and so the five of them would have a traditional high tea of a main course followed by bread and butter, then perhaps scones or cherry buns.

'Though Mum wasn't very much into baking, the Christmas cake was a huge enterprise: Mum baked it months in advance then I got to help with the icing, which was a big treat. After the marzipan and icing were put on I decorated the cake with all the little bits and pieces from the decorating tin. I made it into a real winter wonderland scene. When it came to actually eating it, though, because I hate marzipan, I would have to deconstruct it, removing all vestiges of marzipan and then "rebuilding" my slice by layering on the icing and my little decorative bits once more!'

Because her parents were both French teachers, as she grew older and the great-aunt was no longer with them they took to 'funny foreign ways', such as having cheese in the middle of the meal before pudding – outrageous in those days! Catherine's mum also was ahead of her time as she made her own yoghurt by combining a small tin of Carnation milk with a spoonful of live yoghurt and hot water. This was put into a wide thermos flask overnight and in the morning, yoghurt was ready for breakfast, to be eaten with jam.

Some of Catherine's favourite dishes were sausages and mashed tatties at home, but from the baker's, the big treat was a bag of Aberdeen's famous butteries. 'I loved the way the paper bag of butteries soon took on a transparent sheen as it became seeped in fat. I also used to love Mother's Pride bread, especially the thick end piece. I would love that spread with Echo margarine and often had it when I came in from school. I also used to love sweets. I could make peppermint creams by mixing icing sugar, peppermint essence and water together, rolling into balls then chilling. I also used to love boiling up a can of condensed milk until it became fudge then eating it with a spoon straight from the can.'

At the corner of their road was a sweet shop and Catherine used to go there and buy Sports Mixture (hard fruit gums) – four for a penny. These would be hoarded, along with some end slices of Mother's Pride, in their shed in the garden as her secret stash, 'just in case I wasn't ever fed again!'

They ate out seldom, but when they did, it would be classic fare of the era: prawn cocktail, gammon with pineapple then Black Forest gâteau. They went on occasion to the Allan Water Café in Bridge of Allan for the big treat of buying a fish supper (sometimes white pudding suppers) to take home. 'Even now, passing a chip shop on a cold dark winter night is such a Proustian moment: the smell takes me right back to my childhood, running along the road with my brother with the fish suppers ready to be put into the oven to keep warm.'

There were few things Catherine hated, but amongst those were definitely 'anything offal-y'; tripe in particular she disliked. She also loathed junket.

Another thing she adored, though, was baking cherry buns, which she also loved eating raw. 'Having tried to cram as many cherries into the mixture as I could, I then tried not to scrape the bowl as I was spooning the mixture into the baking tin, as then there was the wonderful act of licking the bowl. I loved the raw mixture. Then the actual buns seemed to bake very fast. These were satisfyingly speedy buns!'

Cherry Buns
makes 10

55g/2 oz soft margarine
55g/2 oz caster sugar
1 large egg

110g/4 oz self-raising flour, sifted
as many glacé cherries as humanly possible (approx. 100g/3½ oz)

Cream together the margarine and sugar, add the egg, then sift in the flour. Beat together well then stir in the cherries.

Spoon into a greased bun tin and bake in an oven preheated to 180°C/350°F/Gas 4 for 12–15 minutes.

Nell Nelson, broadcaster
born 1963

Nell's earliest childhood food memory growing up in North Berwick and Edinburgh was her mother's mince and tatties with tinned carrots. Both her parents loved food: 'My father was always buying my mother cookery books and I loved reading them – aged nine I was the one keen to make Grand Marnier soufflé, not my busy mother!'

Nowadays she still craves that mince of old: 'I love mince and tatties – it's my comfort food – and when I came back from Hong Kong after I lived there, I'd always ask for this – and also Queen of Puddings. Also, my mother made Chinese chicken from a recipe from the *Scotsman* circa 1970, when soy sauce was a strange ingredient, and the deep-fried chicken pieces were sweetened with orange cordial. When I eventually got to Hong Kong, I never tasted anything like my Scottish introduction to Chinese cooking!

'Fish suppers I never got into, but what I did remember having was "a poke of chips" with thick brown sauce after I'd been swimming in North Berwick's unheated swimming pool in May.'

Nell hated both cabbage and Brussels sprouts as a child, but apart from those, she ate most things. She even started to learn to cook at home: 'I learned to cook lots of things, from Elizabeth David to the first *How to Cheat at Cooking* by Delia. I remember making a lovely strawberry and cream mousse.' These days, Nell still loves making some Scottish dishes such as soup, porridge and oatmeal biscuits.

She has very fond memories of her mum's Black Bun at New Year. 'I love Mum's Black Bun – really spicy, made with lots of black pepper and sherry!

'Every year my mother makes Black Bun it is different – the spices vary, so do taste it as you go along and be heavy handed with the pepper and the ginger! It does not have the cloying sweetness of Christmas cake; the pastry case's function in life is to hold in all that delicious, dark, spicy fruit.'

Black Bun

makes 1 bun

Black Bun is a rich, spicy mixture of dried fruit enclosed in a shortcrust pastry. It was originally baked for Twelfth Night but later transferred to Hogmanay, when it is popular as a 'first foot' greeting.

This recipe is from my mum, Jean, and she inherited it from her mother. The dark, peppery fruit warms you up on a cold January morning – along with a wee dram of whisky or sherry, of course.

For the pastry:
350g/12 oz plain flour
½ tsp baking powder
175g/6 oz butter or margarine

75g/2¾ oz sugar (optional)
1 beaten egg
1 egg, for glazing

For the spicy filling:
450g/1 lb stoned raisins (washed and dried)
450g/1 lb currants (washed and dried)
rum, brandy or milk, to soak
225g/8 oz plain flour
½ tsp each of baking soda and cream
   of tartar
1 tsp each of cloves or cinnamon, ginger
   and allspice

½ tsp black pepper
75g/2¾ oz butter (melted)
100g/3½ oz Demerara sugar
1 tbsp syrup or treacle
50g/1¾ oz flaked or chopped almonds
50g/1¾ oz mixed peel orange and
   lemon

Pre-soak the fruit for the filling overnight in the rum, brandy or milk.

First make the pastry. Sift together the flour and baking powder. Rub in the butter or margarine and add the sugar, if using. Mix with beaten egg to form a stiff dough. Roll out thinly. Use two-thirds of the pastry to line a greased cake tin (19cm x 8cm/7½ in x 3¼ in), and the remaining third to form a cover for the filling.

Next, make the filling. Sift the flour, baking soda and cream of tartar and spices into a mixing bowl. Stir in the butter, sugar, syrup or treacle, soaked fruit, nuts and peel. Mix together, turn into the lined tin and press down well. Cover with the prepared lid of pastry and seal the edges well. Prick all over and brush with egg. Pierce with a skewer in 4 places right down to the base. Bake for 2–3 hours in an oven preheated to 140°C/275°F/Gas 1. Test with a skewer in the centre – the bun is ready if it comes out clean. Leave to cool in the tin for 30 minutes on a wire tray until cold. Wrap in greaseproof paper and foil and store in a cool dry place for 3–5 weeks.

Denis Law, footballer
born 1940

Denis Law never realised there was such a thing as a main course, as he only ever had soup and pudding for the family's daily meal. It was only on a Saturday that things looked up. 'My dad was a fisherman – a trawlerman – and each Saturday he would come back after a week away with fresh fish. We would have fresh haddock and home-made chips, which was definitely my favourite meal.'

Growing up in Aberdeen in the 1940s meant that there was not much food around, and since he was youngest of seven children, his mum just produced whatever she could for the family. There was, of course, mince and tatties to supplement the soups, such as tattie or vegetable soup. 'But third-day broth was the worst, so thick you could hardly get your spoon through it!' Puddings were usually something simple like a roly-poly pudding with jam in the middle and custard on top. They also had bread dipped in sugar or, for a treat, bread with syrup.

'We lived on fish and chips, and on special occasions we would go and sit in at the chippy. I can remember sitting there and they would bring us the giant salt cellar and the bottle of brown vinegar.'

Denis hated semolina as a child, with or without jam; he also loathed porridge. 'Even though as a Scotsman I should like it, I just never liked porridge.'

The only thing he ever learned to 'cook' as a child was toast, but that was done in the old-fashioned way with a toasting fork in front of the fire. 'I can still remember burning my hands almost every time.'

When he visits Aberdeen from his home down south, Denis always buys as many mealie (white) puddings, black pudding and rowies (Aberdeen butteries) to take home. 'The mealie puddings we will have on top of mince and tatties when we are back home. And I try to buy as many rowies as I can (at least three dozen) to bring home, depending on baggage space! We used to have rowies a lot as children, eaten only with butter – or, in fact, more usually margarine.

'My mum baked very little, and if she did it was usually something simple like little fairy cakes with icing on top, but my all-time favourite were chocolate cornflake cakes, which to us were such a very special treat!'

Chocolate Cornflake Cakes
makes 12

Sue says: I hope Denis approves of my recipe here.

55g/2 oz butter
4 tbsp golden syrup

2 rounded tbsp cocoa, sifted
100g/3½ oz cornflakes

Melt together the first 3 ingredients, then gently stir in the cornflakes and spoon the mixture into little paper cases. Place in the fridge to chill and firm up.

Edi Stark, broadcaster
born 1955

Edi Stark's first memory of food was being given a ginger biscuit by her dad to stop her crying. 'It was my first solid food and my dad, who was clueless, thought that might make me stop. As I was teething, it was ideal and I stopped crying. I have loved ginger biscuits ever since!' Another early memory again involved her dad: 'I was about three years old and had been ill with flu for a few days and not eating, but one evening I said I'd like to eat crisps. My dad went to peel some potatoes, sliced them really thinly and deep-fried them and they were delicious.

'Food was important to our family, and every day at primary school in Edinburgh my sister and I would go home for lunch and the four of us would sit down to a proper lunch. There was always home-made soup, then twice a week we had fish, which I loathed. Whenever I saw George the fishmonger's van from Port Seton at the house I would despair, as the fish ended up overcooked and full of bones. But there were lots of nice dishes such as fish pie with a breadcrumb topping instead of mashed potatoes, macaroni cheese, mince and tatties, or stew. Tinned peas were usually served, though my mum would regularly get her fresh veg – carrots, potatoes, turnips – from Baillie's the greengrocer's.'

Her mum sometimes cooked more adventurous dishes when Edi was a little older: stuffed peppers or orange and tarragon chicken, possibly followed by a hazelnut meringue with raspberries, all of which became part of her repertoire when they had visitors. And since her dad loved to visit the Italian deli Valvona & Crolla in Edinburgh, they sometimes had proper spaghetti (when everyone else was eating tinned). Her mum was a good baker and Edi remembers great scones, shortbread, Victoria sponge, chocolate Krispies, lemon meringue pie and coconut balls. 'My mum was famous for her coconut balls. We loved them – they were like a round Bounty bar!'

Edi's favourite dishes were roast chicken with bread sauce, roast potatoes and Brussels sprouts, which she still loves. 'Mum did roast potatoes regularly for a while, then she would stop once she had cleaned the cooker; she didn't want the roasting splatters tarnishing her lovely clean oven!'

They had a Hungarian lady living opposite and since they had no TV, Edi was allowed to watch it at her house sometimes. Occasionally she would have afternoon tea there with her mum. 'The cakes Mrs Nodge made (her proper name was Mrs Nagy but we couldn't pronounce that) were amazing, really intricate – the chestnut cakes involved boiling and peeling dozens and dozens of chestnuts.'

She also remembers visiting her maternal granny at weekends and being led out to the garden by her grandfather to collect the tiniest little potatoes especially for her, then picking and podding peas which were all so delicious when cooked.

The family seldom ate out, though Edi remembers one occasion at Patrick Thomson's, the department store on The Bridges. 'We had fish and chips and peas. Whereas at home tomato ketchup was rationed because it was expensive, I remember my dad saying to my sister and me, "You can have as much tomato sauce as you like!" Another time they had gone to a Chinese restaurant and she remembers the surprisingly sweet taste of tinned lychees, which looked to her like pickled onions.

'I never learned to cook at home, only bake. But in my first year at James Gillespie's High School when I was twelve, we had to do a cooking test. We knew we would be tested on either scones or raspberry buns. I practised the buns and, typically, on the day we had to make the scones. I could not remember the recipe and so asked Janet Stewart opposite me how much milk to put in; she refused to tell me so I added far too much liquid then had to add far too much flour to make the dough. They were a disaster and I failed – miserably!'

Nowadays Edi loves to cook Scottish dishes such as cullen skink, stovies (made with lamb and served with thyme-roasted beetroots and oatcakes), mince and tatties, haggis, Atholl Brose and cranachan. She also still loves to make her childhood favourite of roast chicken, bread sauce, roast potatoes and sprouts (nowadays with chestnuts) and her mum's fish pie with the crumb topping.

Coconut Balls
makes 18–20

115g/4 oz unsalted butter, softened
115g/4 oz icing sugar, sifted
175g/6 oz desiccated coconut

½ x 400g tin of condensed milk
250–300g/9–10 oz quality chocolate
(half dark, half milk)

Cream the butter, mix in the sugar, coconut and milk. Mix well and roll into 18–20 balls. Place on greaseproof paper on a baking tray and put it in the fridge for an hour. (Sue says: I place the uncoated balls in the freezer for 20 minutes or so which makes it easier to coat in the chocolate.)

Remove the tray from the freezer, melt the chocolate and, using 2 forks, dip in the coconut balls. Place each chocolate-coated ball on a sheet of greaseproof paper to set.

Sharman Macdonald, playwright
born 1951

Sharman Macdonald vividly recalls when she was only eighteen months old and being forced to eat mince and potatoes. For three or four days she was given this loathed dish for breakfast, lunch and tea, always served in one of her grandmother's blue willow patterned plates. On the final day, when Sharman's mother gave in and fed her what her finicky daughter actually liked – chicken soup and strained apples – a friend who was a hospital matron chided her with a scathing 'That child has beaten you!'

Sharman's mother was a fabulous cook and everything was home-made. Her trifles were legendary and every New Year's Day, which they spent at Sharman's Uncle Bill's, her mother would always take a trifle. This was, however, another dish young Sharman disliked. But she absolutely adored fish cakes, made with tinned tuna. These were served on Thursdays with potato crisps: 'We were not allowed to eat the crisps with our fingers so had to manipulate them between the prongs of a fork!'

During her childhood in Edinburgh she also recalls loving home-made potato croquettes, served with roast lamb on a Sunday, and also her mother's baking: Empire biscuits, shortbread, Victoria sponge, chocolate cake (her mum's was 'amazing') and 'fly cemetery'. 'When she made gypsy creams I remember helping her by kneading it gently in the bowl into a breaky pastry consistency, then rolling a teaspoonful of the mixture lightly into a ball before slightly flattening it onto the greased floured tray, but only slightly. Sandwiched together they were quite a mouthful. We used to split them and lick out the cream.'

There was so much sugar in those days, she recalled: 'I remember having freshly squeezed orange juice, which was of course healthy but it was served with three teaspoons of sugar in it! I used to love tipping the glass up at the end and sucking up the sugar. And my mother's cure for a cough at night-time was to make butterballs: balls of butter rolled in sugar... I can remember them all laid out in a circle round a saucer!' There were also pancakes fresh from the girdle, or griddle, spread with just butter or butter and lemon curd.

Because she was a fussy eater, Sharman and her mother had many battles over food: though she loved most soups (and still loves to make them with good home-made stock), she disliked mushroom soup and remembers huge fights over it. However, so cowed was she by one particular mother–daughter fight that when her mum forgot to put the sugar in the rhubarb crumble, Sharman and her dad just ate it, tart and unpleasant though it was!

With her own children (Caleb and Keira Knightly), Sharman refused point blank to ever force them to eat, given her memories of food fights with her own mum. When they were growing up, she did cook them mince but never simply with potatoes – more often spaghetti Bolognese or chilli con carne. One other thing she loathed as she was growing up was porridge, but her husband Will used to make it just for himself and for Keira, who loves porridge, albeit taken in the more southern way, with sugar, not salt.

Though she occasionally had fish and chips, Sharman disliked chip-shop chips as her mother's home-made chips were so good. And though her grandmother made crinkly chips, her mother's were smooth-edged and often served with lamb gigot chops. Cooked in beef dripping, these were wonderful. She remembers her dad doing some cooking too: 'He used to cook curries – a magnificent red curry – in a bucket over a primus stove in the back garden, not only because of the (albeit fabulous) smell going through the house, but also, he simply liked cooking outside.'

Sharman remembers dipping not only raw rhubarb but also raw gooseberries into bowls of sugar in the garden. 'I also remember black treacle sandwiches on white bread. It's a wonder we are all still here, we ate so much sweet stuff! Unusually, though, my grandfather used to eat strawberries not dipped into sugar, but with salt and pepper!'

Hogmanay was a special day, with First Footers coming to their house for the food her mum had prepared: boiled ham, rolled tongue, a great spread and plenty of home baking. Then, once the First Footing was done, everyone would congregate at their house again for breakfast at 6am; but for Sharman, definitely no porridge!

Gypsy Creams
makes 10

A brief recipe... I'm guessing a bit because the ink's run in my mother's old recipe book and the page is very yellow. Once upon a time I knew it off by heart.

They should be rounded when they come out of the oven and, of course, then be sandwiched together. They don't necessarily look wonderfully attractive – but the taste... Sod Proust and his Madeleines! This is so much better – the taste of a small sweet sin.

55g/2 oz margarine or butter
55g/2 oz lard
55g/2 oz caster sugar
100g/3½ oz/1 cup porridge oats

115g/4 oz/1 cup plain flour
2 tsp cocoa powder
2 tsp syrup
2 tbsp hot water

For the filling:
55g/2 oz margarine or butter
100g/3½ oz icing sugar, sifted

2 tsp cocoa, sifted

Cream the fats and sugar together. Add the porridge oats, flour and cocoa, then the syrup and water. Combine gently then drop teaspoonfuls onto a greased baking sheet (about 20).

Bake in an oven preheated to 180°C/350°F/Gas 4 for 15 minutes. Remove to a wire rack to cool.

Meanwhile, make the filling. Beat together all the ingredients until smooth, then use to sandwich together 2 biscuits.

Sue says: This recipe really does work, even though Sharman 'guessed at it'!

Mike Blair, rugby player
born 1981

When Mike Blair was growing up in Edinburgh, the food his mum prepared for the family of four boys was – even then – very much geared round rugby. His dad played rugby and liked spaghetti Bolognese before a game, so the family would eat that often. On a Sunday evening, after the traditional Sunday roast at lunchtime, his dad would cook spaghetti carbonara, one of the few things he made, but a great family favourite. With six of them eating together there was always plenty of Yorkshire puddings with the roast, too, and always some kind of dessert such as Eve's pudding, apple crumble or fruit salad.

Mike adored macaroni cheese and still does, though he admits his wife Viv, a vegetarian, makes it better than he does now. When they were first dating, Mike used to make his mum's macaroni cheese and put a pizza in the oven too; now, Viv's macaroni cheese has overtaken Mike's in excellence. Indeed, if he has played an important game of rugby and the team has lost, his wife texts him to say 'Macaroni cheese tonight!' since it is his favourite comfort food.

As for dislikes, Mike had a few: 'When we used to ask Mum what we were eating that night, she would say "Surprise Pie". When we asked what was in that, she was vague, as it was one of my most hated foods, fish pie. And that, along with anything else sloppy – porridge, semolina, rice pudding – I have never liked.'

His granny made very good suet pudding and also excellent strawberry ice cream: this latter is something he still craves, it was so good. She made this – and lots of jams, too – from the many berries (strawberries, raspberries and loganberries) in the garden. 'Since Granny covered everything, like home-made marmalades and jams, Mum never felt she needed to make them at home.'

The family did not eat out much except on holiday, and on one he recalls an incredible seven-course dinner one night in a hotel in Guernsey. They never had takeaways, apart from the occasional fish supper, but this was usually on the way home from somewhere. Saturday evening had a routine to it: 'As we all loved to watch *Gladiators* and *Baywatch*, we would pop trays of fish fingers, waffles and pizza into the oven and eat those with beans as a treat.'

Mike's mum was very good at soups: 'Her best is probably carrot soup, though she also did broths, and this was a big thing on a Saturday. In the last year of school, there would be rugby training until 12pm then I would take four or five of my friends back to my house where Mum would feed us all soup or pasta before the match at 2.30pm.'

Every New Year's Day there was butcher's steak pie – same thing every year – and the family all sat together round the table. There was also a routine to everyday meals. 'Mum had a kind of rotation with dishes such as the loathed Surprise Pie, a casseroley thing, macaroni cheese, carbonara, mince and tatties and breaded haddock (this latter with mashed potatoes and peas) and she also made a wonderful rice dish of peas and bacon which was not a risotto but equally delicious.'

One of Mike's favourite Scottish dishes is haggis, and at his wedding, that was the starter – regular meat haggis for the groom, vegetarian for the bride. Simple, really!

Another of Mike's favourites from childhood was his mum's flapjacks. They were – and still are – legendary.

Flapjacks
makes 12–16

175g/6 oz butter or margarine
1 heaped tbsp golden syrup
115g/4 oz Demerara sugar

225g/8 oz porridge oats
pinch of salt

Melt the first 3 ingredients together then stir in the oats. (Sue says: I add a good pinch of salt at this stage.)

Combine well then tip into a 20cm/8 in, square, lightly greased baking tin. Bake in an oven preheated to 180°C/350°F/Gas 4 for about 20 minutes or until golden brown. Mark into squares while warm, but only remove from the tray when they are cold.

Sir Tom Farmer, entrepreneur and philanthropist
born 1940

When Tom Farmer was growing up in Leith, the area of Edinburgh beside the docks, his abiding memory was of tripe. Monday was wash day, but also tripe day, and Tom used to love it – his mum's tripe was thick and soup-like, with plenty of onions. Later in his life, when he married and had his own family, they would all go to his mum's on Sunday and the special treat was to have tripe. When Mrs Farmer died, one of her friends brought Tom a jar of tripe after Mass on Sundays, as she knew he would be missing not only his mum but also her tripe!

Mince also featured heavily in Tom's diet, as feeding seven children (Tom was the youngest) meant thrift was essential – and there was still post-war rationing. There was also a dish called 'rodiken', which is dark tripe: his mother used to put the rodiken and oatmeal into a sheep's stomach, boil it up and serve it. 'Mum told us all it was haggis but the family called it rodiken – it filled us all up.' There was also an abundance of soups, particularly potato soup. And stovies, too, made with onions, potatoes and sausages, though sometimes corned beef would be served alongside. We sometimes went to the cinema on a Saturday night then got fish suppers on the way home – a real treat.'

But, incongruously, even though the family was large Tom says 'we never wanted for anything'. Indeed, they often had luxuries too, on account of his dad's job as shipping agent at the docks. Every Christmas they had turkey, which was perhaps unusual for Leith, and even more surprising, they had caviar: 'Dad would bring home tins of caviar and the seven of us kids would sit round the kitchen table in Leith and eat a spoonful on toast. One time we even fed it to the cat!'

Cloutie dumping was another great dish his mum made, a great pudding boiled in a cloth. His grandmother, who lived nearby, would make special dumplings for birthdays with silver threepennies in them; his mum's were without pennies, though still delicious.

Tom reckons his mum must have worked an eighteen-hour day simply looking after the family, always cooking. When he got up in the morning she was in the kitchen cooking and when he went to bed at night she was still doing housework. She would regularly bake simple things like scones (though invariably buy the Black Bun and shortbread for New Year) but her home-baked melting moments were a great family favourite.

Melting Moments
makes 12

55g/2 oz butter
40g/1½ oz caster sugar
1 tsp vanilla essence

70g/2½ oz self-raising flour
rolled oats, for coating
glacé cherries (optional)

Mix the butter, sugar and vanilla essence together, then stir in the flour and mix thoroughly.

Divide the mixture into approximately 12 small balls, and coat with rolled oats. Place on a greased baking tray, flatten slightly and, for decoration, a glacé cherry can be added on the centre of each biscuit, if you like.

Bake in an oven preheated to 180°C/350°F/Gas 4 for about 10–15 minutes. Remove from the oven and leave on the tray for a couple of minutes, then transfer them to a wire rack to cool.

Kaye Adams, broadcaster
born 1962

'My earliest childhood memory is one I told my daughter about... stupidly. I can remember at a very early age making butterballs. Blobs of butter rolled in sugar: and we ate them! My teeth ache at the thought of them now but my five-year-old thinks they sound delicious,' Kaye tells me. And describing how she grew up in Grangemouth, she says, 'We were far from foodies. My mum worked full time and so had no time to experiment or cook for fun, so food was functional. My granny was a very good baker. She made a lovely Victoria sponge and blackberry and apple jelly, which I loved.'

Kaye's favourite childhood dish was mince and tatties; she still craves it, but since nowadays she is a fish-eating vegetarian, it's a bit tricky to eat it! From time to time she makes quorn mince and tatties, but she reckons it's not the same. As a child, she ate out sometimes: 'At Berni Inns we would have prawn cocktail, steak and baked potato followed by Black Forest gâteau.' They also did high tea on a Sunday quite a lot and she recalls 'ploughing through fish and chips and peas just to get to the cakes at the end'.

She loathed liver as a child and tells me just how strong this hatred was: 'At one school I went to, they served it every week and every week I would leave the dining room with a piece of gravy-sodden liver in my blazer pocket. By the end of term, there were living organisms camping in there!'

Nowadays, the most Scottish thing she cooks is lentil soup or Scotch broth (with no meat), as she loves soup. She also loves Scottish shellfish and Arbroath Smokies, but another meaty memory is of Sunday: 'Every Sunday we had a piece of silverside. I've no idea what that is, apart from a lump of beef, but we had it every Sunday in life!'

Millionaire's Shortbread

makes 24 pieces

Sue says: Kaye's friend Shirley Blair's mum was a wonderful baker and Kaye used to watch her make this glorious stuff 'barely able to contain my excitement'. Hopefully my recipe will hit the spot too!

For the shortbread base:
175g/6 oz plain flour
75g/2¾ oz cornflour
75g/2¾ oz golden caster sugar

175g/6 oz slightly salted butter,
　　slightly softened

For the caramel and topping:
2 x 400g tins of condensed milk

300g/10½ oz quality chocolate
　　(half milk, half plain)

Sift the flours into a food processor, add the caster sugar and then butter, then whiz briefly to bring the mixture together into a ball. Remove from the processor and knead it lightly.

Press the mixture into a lightly greased Swiss-roll tin that is 33cm x 23cm/13 in x 9 in, and press flat. Prick with a fork and bake in an oven preheated to 180°C/350°F/Gas 4 for about 25 minutes or until golden brown. Cool in the tin.

To make the caramel, place the unopened cans of milk on their sides in a heavy saucepan and cover with boiling water; the water should almost cover the tins. Cover and simmer for 2 hours, checking now and then, topping up with more boiling water if necessary. Remove the cans and leave to cool completely before opening and spreading carefully over the base. Leave until cold.

Finally, melt the chocolate then spread it over the caramel. Cut into 24 squares once set.

Fred Macaulay, broadcaster and comedian
born 1956

Fred's first memory involving food was aged about three or four in Callander, where the family used to live. He recalls opening the blue twisted paper of salt and shaking them all over Smith's crisps! But their next move (Fred's dad was the village Bobby so they moved often) was to Rattray in Perthshire, and here he recalls his mum's mutton broth. It was not only served for Fred, his brother and sister, but also to visitors such as the snowplough team who had been called in by Fred's dad, and were frozen after many hours' work clearing snow. 'I also remember being given a tablespoon of malt, which I presume came from Dewar's, the local whisky company: the texture was not dissimilar to treacle and this was something that was taken under sufferance as it was more medicinal than tasty.'

Because of his dad's job as a policeman, the Macaulay family were lucky to often be given trout, salmon, pheasant and even goose: 'Some were gifts, some were evidence.' Once when the Canadian relatives came to stay, his mum apologised that 'all' they had for tea was trout and pheasant! The trout was from Loch Dungarthill, the salmon from the River Ericht and the birds from nearby farms and estates. The geese were so big that you could cut off the breasts and cook them just like steaks, grilled. Fred remembers the cleaning and gutting and plucking of the pheasants in the kitchen before they were served, roasted.

Back to more traditional fare, though, and Fred remembers the cloutie dumpling and its linen shroud being removed so the classic skin could form. 'I also recall the "jeely bag" dripping with apple jelly, suspended on broom handles over an upturned stool.' His mum made jam from the raspberries and strawberries in the garden and he can still remember not only the wonderful smell, but also the pounds and pounds of sugar coming into the kitchen when it was jam time.

Mince and tatties was another favourite, of course, although Fred told me about one time before a school party that he had to eat mince but it had carrots in it, which he loathed. When told he would not be going to the party unless he ate his mince, he remembers making the decision not to go to the party! Oatmeal was also added to the mince to eke it out, but none of the three children liked it, so his mum soon stopped that experiment. Stovies were well loved, enhanced only with mutton or lamb; the first time he saw someone put sausages in stovies, he was horrified and thought it sacrilege.

The family never ate out, apart from the occasional fish suppers after their Thursday night's swimming at the Perth Baths. Their Uncle Richard once introduced them to the new Chinese restaurant in Blairgowrie, only to be embarrassed by the order: one Chinese, five steaks!

At school dinners Fred had to sit with seven fellow pupils and one teacher at a table. When a pudding was served with custard (chocolate sponge always came with pink strawberry custard), the teacher offered the custard round but everyone refused, which meant the teacher had to take it first from the jug and therefore have to take the thick globby layer of congealed skin. Once that had gone, however, suddenly seven pupils wanted custard. 'Once he cottoned onto this trick, though, the teacher sat eating custard-swathed pudding with one hand, the jug in the other, while we all sat with dry sponge in front of us!'

Fred's mum was a good cook and, like so many other Scottish mums, good at soups. As well as lentil soup and broths, she made lettuce soup, as Fred's dad grew lettuce in the garden. When I asked Fred if it was Vichyssoise-style, he replied, 'No, we were far too traditional for cold soups: this was simply a combination of onions softened in butter, lettuce added and wilted, then all covered in stock, liquidised and served in true Macaulay family style with a dod of cream!'

But it was his mum's shortbread that was legendary. To Fred and his family, her recipe is still the best.

Shortbread
makes 20–24 pieces

Sue says: I was lucky enough to have been given Fred's mum's famous recipe years ago.

225g/8 oz butter (slightly salted), softened
115g/4 oz caster sugar
225g/8 oz plain flour, sifted

150g/5½ oz cornflour, sifted
caster sugar, to dredge

Place the butter and sugar in a mixer or food processor and cream until pale. Once well amalgamated, add the flour and cornflour and blend briefly, just until thoroughly combined.

Tip into a buttered Swiss-roll tin (23cm x 33cm/9 in x 13 in) and, using floured hands, press down so it is level. Prick all over (do this carefully so that you do not disturb the level surface) then bake in an oven preheated to 150°C/300°F/Gas 2 for 50–60 minutes.

What you are looking for is a uniform pale golden colour – do not allow it to become golden brown. Remove and dredge with caster sugar then cut into squares. Leave for 5 minutes or so, then carefully decant onto a wire rack to cool.

Maggie O'Farrell, novelist
born 1972

Maggie O'Farrell vividly recalls Sundays in North Berwick, where the family moved when she was twelve, eating freshly made drop scones (Scotch pancakes) in front of the fire while watching *The Dukes of Hazzard* on TV. This was after her parents had been to their Quakers meeting in the morning and then had the family lunch of casserole which had been simmering in the oven all morning. All in all, a very traditional Sunday.

Another tradition she remembers was Hallowe'en. Because she has Irish parents, this was hugely important as she grew up: there was dooking for apples but also a special Hallowe'en Barm Brack, a rich sweetened bread studded with dried fruit and peel. In it were hidden foil-wrapped charms, such as a wedding ring (this meant the person who got it would be married that year), a nut (they would have a baby), a button or a coin (they would be poor or rich).

The Barm Brack was always home-made, as Maggie's mum is a great baker. She always had tins full of cakes, tea loaves, scones, rock cakes, Selkirk bannock and flapjacks, as in a town like North Berwick people popped in for a quick visit regularly. When Maggie was about thirteen she worked in a greasy spoon in the town, and though she was serving 'a lot of baked beans and toasties made with bright orange Cheddar (I had never seen cheese so orange!),' all the cakes were baked in-house, so she became acquainted with that rather Scottish phenomenon, the traybake, from millionaire's shortbread to tiffin. They also made good scones – cheese and plain – and she remembers being flummoxed by 'an old lady coming in one day and asking for a scone that was "not well fired"'. 'Well fired' might be common parlance to those having spent their entire childhood in Scotland, but for Maggie arriving only aged twelve, it was a mystery!

When she was about fourteen, Maggie worked in a hotel where she served more upmarket Scottish fare; from salmon to cranachan. But it was the soup that brought back vivid memories: 'An American ordered the cullen skink then called me over and complained it was far too thick. The chef was rather a cross man anyway and so did not take kindly to the request and refused point blank to do anything about it, so I had to return it, unaltered, to the irate customer.' Nowadays, although Maggie is a vegetarian, she loves fish (her mum used to buy fish from North Berwick harbour in the 1980s – cod, haddock and crab) and now she loves to make cullen skink, perhaps just a little thinner than she recalls from childhood.

School dinners were not good, although she used to enjoy haggis (she only became a vegetarian aged sixteen) and puddings with custard. But it was in school years she discovered the joys of Tunnock's Caramel Wafers, Tea Cakes and Macaroon bars. She also recalls going to the baker after school for a 'Macaroni Pie', sometimes having that with chips: 'What a starch fest! Or I might have a fish supper as a treat, followed perhaps by an Oyster (ice cream between two oyster shells) from the Italian ice-cream shops. There is a huge Italian influence on Scottish cuisine,' she told me, 'although at home we only ever had pasta once when I was growing up. But my grandmother, aged ninety-three, is proud to claim she has never eaten pasta to this day!'

Maggie's dad had an allotment at the foot of the garden and grew lots of vegetables – mainly potatoes (though broad beans also featured and Maggie still loathes them) and fruit, from redcurrants and rhubarb to apples. Her mum made jam – raspberry, strawberry, rhubarb and ginger – every year. And indeed when Maggie lived in London, she and her Scottish friend Morag would ask each other when visiting family to bring back down rhubarb and ginger jam and also Simmers biscuits, which they both adored.

But now, living in Edinburgh, Maggie stirs up memories of her childhood by making drop scones – though not only on Sundays, and never in front of the TV!

Sunday Afternoon Drop Scones
(Scotch Pancakes)

makes 24–30

I asked my mother to write out this recipe for me recently because I wanted to make them for my son. She used to make these drop scones for me and my sisters and we would eat them in front of the fire, while watching *The Dukes of Hazzard*. The slightly burnt, sweetish taste is now permanently and oddly associated with law-dodging men in tight denim and noisy cars.

7 dessertspoons plain flour

2 dessertspoons sugar

1 tsp cream of tartar

½ tsp bicarbonate of soda

1 egg

milk

Mix all the dry ingredients together then mix to a thick batter by adding the egg and a few drops of milk.

Drop a few tablespoonfuls of the batter at a time onto a hot, greased girdle, or griddle (or failing that, a frying pan). When golden brown, turn them over and cook them on the other side. They can be kept warm in a tea towel, if you like, but they are actually better eaten as you go along, plain or spread with raspberry jam.

Alexander McCall Smith, author
born 1948

Alexander McCall Smith's first memories of food are of eating cake at a birthday party when he was about four years old. But since he was brought up in what was then called Southern Rhodesia, albeit with a Scottish father, food was a little different from what others were used to. As there was a lot of maize grown (the Zimbabwean staple is still maizemeal porridge) he often had fresh corn on the cob with butter – and with the everyday fare of roast beef and peas he would have boiled pumpkin, this latter an unknown vegetable in Scotland during the 1950s.

But every single day of his childhood he had porridge, then either bacon and eggs or sometimes kippers. He had plain Scottish fare such as mince and tatties, but also more unusual dishes: brains; and tripe and onions done in a milky sauce was one of his all-time favourites, too. Most food was prepared by their cook, who rustled up excellent egg and potato pie – and macaroni cheese was deemed 'the height of sophistication!' As for sweet things, his mother made wonderful coconut ice. 'There was always fruit cake', Alexander told me, 'and sponge fingers which we had with custard. We had a lot of custard, almost daily in fact – and semolina pudding with jam or syrup at least twice a week.'

When he came to Edinburgh as a student, he stayed during the holidays with his aunt on Unst, the most northerly Shetland island. She was an excellent cook and he vividly remembers her wonderful soups (she took a lot of time making proper stocks), good roast lamb, oatcakes, mealie puddings, herring in oatmeal, rollmops, and especially trout – his aunt was an angler and so not only cooked but also caught the fish. 'One of the most unusual dishes I had up there were tatties cooked in seawater. They were very good and tasted so fresh.'

Food played a part in the long journey to get to his aunt's house in Unst in the first instance. His memory of butteries (known as rowies to Aberdonians) is strong: 'Getting off the Aberdeen boat in Lerwick in the early morning after an awful journey – cold and uncomfortable – then going to a café made of tin (it must have blown away by now!), getting a mug of tea and a butterie delivered from heaven.' To him, one of the most delicious things he has ever eaten.

As a student, Alexander had to learn to cook and his 'flat's specials' were such dishes as bully beef with rice or potatoes and tinned peas. Sometimes they would add garlic powder to a dish to make it truly sophisticated! Nowadays, though, he enjoys cooking, but mainly Mediterranean-style dishes using Scottish ingredients. Kippers from Pittenweem are a favourite and he sources superb smoked salmon: 'The smoked salmon we get from Archie in Argyll, near Campbeltown, which is specially cured and smoked, is the most delicious thing on the face of the earth.' Well, that and the memory of those Aberdeen butteries in Lerwick!

Butteries
makes 15–16

Sue says: Here is my own recipe for them.

For the bread dough:
450g/1 lb strong flour
20g/¾ oz fresh yeast

40g/1½ oz sugar
approx. 300ml/½ pint water (tepid)

For the fat dough:
250g/9 oz white shortening
75g/2¾ oz lard
40g/1½ oz salt

50g/1¾ oz plain flour, plus extra
    for preparation

First, prepare the fat dough by mixing the 2 fats with the salt and flour and leaving at room temperature so it is soft enough to work with. Next, make the bread dough. Place the flour in a bowl and mix in the sugar and fresh yeast, then mix into the water in another bowl. Combine and knead – by hand or with a dough hook – until smooth (about 10 minutes by hand). Leave to rise for 30–45 minutes then knock back the dough and fold into a rectangle shape.

Divide the fat dough into three and add a third at a time to a third of the bread dough. Then fold over and continue with the remaining thirds. It is a folding process, rather like making puff pastry. Then, using well-floured hands, 'chop' in the fat by hand, using the blade of a blunt knife (or the long edge of a palette knife). Once well combined, the dough is no longer soft and unmanageable but slightly sticky and rough. (You will need lots of flour throughout this preparation.)

Cut into about 15–16 pieces and place these on a baking sheet. Shape them by pressing the front part of your (floured) hand – fingers only – onto each, so they are flattened and dimpled with fingerprints with one stroke. Cover with oiled clingfilm and leave to prove somewhere warm for another 30 minutes or so, then bake in an oven preheated to 220°C/425°F/Gas 7 for 25–30 minutes, until crispy and golden. Remove to a wire rack to cool.

Billy McNeill, footballer
born 1940

When Billy McNeill was growing up in Bellshill, Glasgow, in the 1940s, he had mince and potatoes regularly, just like everyone else. But he also had hearty cabbage soup, Lithuanian-style: his grandfather, his mother's dad, was Lithuanian and as he lived with them ever since Billy's grandmother had died, the food his mother cooked was a combination of basic wholesome Scottish and Lithuanian. So, as well as the wonderful thick cabbage soup, he remembers eating salami decades before most Scots had even heard of it. 'There was also a bucket of brine in the kitchen, filled with fish – mackerel and herring – and also sliced beetroot and onions in it. This was eaten cold. With that we had dark Lithuanian bread called *duona*. It was all very good; but I'd say mince is still my favourite.

'My mother also made other great soups – broth and lentil were the staples. And her baking was excellent. But in those days working-class women had little choice but to be good cooks as they had families to feed on little money.'

The McNeill family only ever ate out if they took a trip down the coast to Troon or Largs and there they would sit in a café and eat fish and chips, with vinegar, white bread and butter and cups of tea.

When I asked if there was anything Billy hated as child he told me, 'No, but the food wasn't that adventurous, it was simple peasant food. It was smashing! And having been brought up with the Lithuanian food too, this held me in good stead when Celtic played in Europe, as I had no apprehensions at all about trying the continental food.'

Hogmanay in Bellshill, an engineering and mining community, was one of the few times people would be seen going from one house to the next for their drams. Billy's family lived in a house in one of the 'miners' rows' and he recalls it being one of the few times people actually drank at home. They would have not only whisky but also, given his heritage, vodka. 'A baker in Mosshead found out about the craving of the Lithuanian community for their black bread and so began to make it especially for them. But he also found out they liked vodka and somehow got that for them too: both were sold in the baker's shop!'

New Year's Day was steak pie with potatoes and cabbage which was very tasty; his Dundonian father loved that dish. And his mother's tablet was yet another all-time favourite of Billy: 'There were very few sweetie shops then and so my mother made it regularly, in long baking trays. I loved it then; and still do now.'

Tablet
makes 24–30 pieces

Sue says: Here is my foolproof tablet recipe, for Billy.

125g/4½ oz unsalted butter
1kg/2 lb 4 oz golden granulated sugar
300ml/10 fl oz full-fat milk

200g/7 oz condensed milk (half a regular can)
2 tsp pure vanilla extract

Place the butter in a large, heavy-based saucepan (only a reliable pan should be used, otherwise it will stick). Melt over a low heat.

Add the sugar, milk and a pinch of salt and heat gently until the sugar is dissolved, stirring occasionally. Once it has dissolved, bring to the boil and simmer over a fairly high heat for 8–10 minutes, stirring.

Add the condensed milk, stir well then simmer for a further 8–10 minutes (it should bubble, but not too fiercely), stirring constantly.

After 8 minutes, test if it is ready. What you want is the 'soft-ball' stage, which means that when you drop a little of the mixture into a cup of very cold water, it will form a soft ball which you can pick up between your fingers. On a sugar thermometer, it should read 240°F/115°C.

At this stage, remove from the heat at once and add the vanilla. Using an electric whisk, beat on medium for 4–5 minutes just until you feel it begin to stiffen a little and become ever so slightly grainy. (You can of course do this by hand but it will take at least 10 minutes and it is hard work!) Pour immediately into a buttered Swiss-roll tin (23cm x 33cm/9 in x 13 in) and allow to cool. Then mark into squares or oblongs when it is almost cold. When completely cold, remove and store in an air-tight tin or wrap individually in waxed paper.

Stephen Jardine, broadcaster
born 1963

Stephen Jardine's first memory is of being four or five years old and having to stay at home with the womenfolk as he was too young to go to the football with the men! 'We used to go to my dad's mum every Saturday for high tea. The men went to the football, and up until the age of about seven or eight, I was too much of a nuisance there, always asking for some lemonade then needing to visit the toilet. So I would be at home while the preparation was going on for my grandmother's wonderful high tea, which would consist of a simple main course – salad, shepherd's pie, smoked fish – followed by a great spread of sweet things. The table literally groaned with pan scones, Victoria sponge filled with raspberry jam, fairy cakes and caramel shortbread. It was a real test to get through the main course without touching any of the sweet things. It was here, I realise now, that I was first introduced to the sense of family and the closeness of eating together.'

Another early memory as he grew up in Dumfries was of coming home from school for lunch. There were always two courses: a main, such as mince and potatoes or stew or tripe and onions (which Stephen loved), and then a pudding such as steamed syrup pudding, apple crumble or a lovely apple and cinnamon pudding called Melva pudding.

His mother was a good traditional cook and fantastic baker; pan scones (Scotch pancakes) were an abiding memory of daily life, not only in his own home but also at his grandmother's at those wonderful Saturday high teas. Nowadays Stephen eats them with local heather honey, but as a child they would only have been spread with butter.

Food was of huge importance in the family: 'Mum spent most of her life cooking, she was an instinctive cook and loved giving joy through food.' Stephen now likes to make pan scones with his son Jack as a continuation of the family food legacy.

Favourite childhood dishes were many, but if he had to choose 'it would be anything with pastry. Mum's shortcrust was the best – I think half butter, half lard. It was perfect – not too short and browned beautifully. Her mince tarts, Eyemouth tart, apple pies and rhubarb tarts were fabulous, but she would also make savoury pies of mince, onions and carrots and the most sublime puff pasty which she used to cover her steak pies. Her sausage rolls and Forfar bridies were also wonderful.' Even now Stephen adores all things to do with pastry because of her, whether a cold pork pie or hot Scotch pie.

Though there was nothing he hated to eat at home, school dinners were dreadful: 'I just have memories of overcooked spinach, tough rubbery liver and gristly meat.'

The family only ate out on special occasions and it was always to the same place, a traditional Italian restaurant called Bruno's in Dumfries. They always had the same thing: his mum would have the antipasti cold meats, his dad the minestrone and Stephen the pasta to start, then they would all have steak. Fish suppers were another occasional treat and when he came to Edinburgh as a student he was introduced to the delights of haggis and black pudding suppers at the L'Alba D'Ora Café.

He learned to cook at home before he went to university: 'Mum insisted I not only learn to make her wonderful pastry, but also mince, chicken stroganoff and a macaroni cheese recipe which had condensed milk in it, rather unusually, and was topped with a crust made from Ruskoline, the orange crumbs used to coat fish for frying.'

Nowadays, he cooks a lot, and in his experiment of eating only Scottish food for an entire year, he and his wife Sheila went back to basics. 'I love reinventing the classics, such as fishcakes made with salmon or smoked haddock, and we make lots of soups such as Scotch broth and vegetable soups. I also make raspberry jam and have rediscovered the joys of baking because I couldn't resort to a Jaffa Cake! As well as the family favourite of pan scones, there are always flapjacks on the go.'

Hogmanay is full of food memories, mainly involving sausage rolls as his mum would make a batch of forty-eight, all with her home-made puff pastry. And there was shortbread – and always trifle. 'I remember when I was seventeen or eighteen coming home very late after First Footing and rather drunk. I ended up eating all the leftovers in the gargantuan bowl that had been filled with Mum's trifle. Strangely, I did not feel very well on New Year's Day!'

Eyemouth Tart

makes 1 tart

175g/6 oz shortcrust pastry
55g/2 oz currants
55g/2 oz chopped walnuts
55g/2 oz coconut
55g/2 oz glacé cherries, quartered

55g/2 oz raisins
25g/1 oz caster sugar
1 large egg, beaten
25g/1 oz butter, melted

For the topping:
225g/8 oz icing sugar

2 tbsp lemon juice

Roll out the pastry and place in a greased Swiss-roll tin (23cm x 33cm/9 in x 13 in).

Mix all the next 6 ingredients together, add the beaten egg and melted butter and spread over the pastry base. Bake in an oven preheated to 190°C/375°F/Gas 5 for about 25 minutes.

For the topping, mix the icing sugar with the lemon juice and a little water and spread over the top. Cut into squares when cool.

Sue says: The filling was doubled for the photo to make it deeper and even more moist. You can also use different colours of glacé cherries, as we did here.

James Naughtie, broadcaster
born 1952

Some of James Naughtie's earliest memories of growing up in rural Aberdeenshire involve eating fruit from the back garden: 'I remember fresh raspberries, strawberries and redcurrants – I can taste them now (especially when, occasionally, I buy the peely-wally imitations from supermarkets).

'My mother was a good, instinctive cook and I grew up on a rich traditional menu – mince and tatties, shimmering Scotch broth, flavoursome stews, chickens (and sometimes rather more mature birds) that had been running around not long before – and fine baking.'

Most of their eating out was done on holidays or shopping trips. 'These trips might be to the metropolis of Aberdeen, as our village didn't have restaurants! But of course there were also fish suppers and all the rest of it from chip shops. In my case, I'm afraid I also loved black pudding suppers [black pudding in batter with chips].

'My dark secret from early childhood is my shaming dislike of fresh fish. When the van came from the Banffshire coast on Friday mornings, I'd turn my nose up at fresh lemon sole. And when my father came back with fresh trout from the River Deveron, I wouldn't touch them. I learned the error of my ways, just in time.'

James likes to do some cooking at home nowadays: 'Sometimes I concoct a blow-out cullen skink that keeps us going for a while. And when I go home to Scotland, I enjoy the best beef in the world and all that fresh fish I once spurned. A special memory, apart from the creaking cake stands, was something my mother did with pheasants, and the fresh vegetables from the garden, eaten in their proper seasons. These scones also remind me of home: warm and comforting and very tasty.'

Buttermilk Fruit Scones
makes about 10

These are easy and delicious, made using only a bowl and a baking tray. If you have a good eye you can even guess the quantities; they don't have to be spot-on.

225g/8 oz self-raising flour
1 tsp baking powder
a large pinch of salt
40g/1½ oz caster sugar

40g/1½ oz butter
50g/1¾ oz sultanas
150ml/5 fl oz buttermilk
        (you can substitute ordinary milk,
        but you'll lose the lightness)

Preheat the oven to 230°C/450°F/Gas 8. Grease a baking sheet, or line it with silicone paper.

Sift the dry ingredients together (or just mix them if you can't be bothered). Rub in the butter until the mixture is like breadcrumbs, then add in the sultanas and distribute through the mixture with your fingers.

Pour in the buttermilk and press everything together into a dough. Don't let it get too wet – it shouldn't stick to your fingers. If it does, add some more flour. If it seems too dry to manipulate, add some more liquid (preferably buttermilk).

You don't need to roll the dough out. Just press it out onto a floured board – not too thin – about 2.5cm/1 in deep.

With a cutter, cut as many rounds as you can. Or you can just separate the dough into 10–12 equal pieces, and gently pat them into scone-like shapes. They'll be rough but homely. Push in any sultanas sticking out from the edges, so that they don't burn. Place the scones on the greased baking sheet, allowing space between them. If you have some flour left over, sprinkle a little across the tops of the scones.

Bake for about 8 minutes or until the scones have risen and turned light brown. Cool them for about 10 minutes, and enjoy immediately.

Chris Paterson, rugby player
born 1978

'My earliest food memory isn't a particularly good one. My main recollection from my early days was that I was a really fussy eater. I can remember sitting at the table in a bad mood picking all the little pieces of onion out of my mince and tatties. I'm happy to say times have changed and I'm no longer a fussy eater. In fact, the opposite.'

Chris Paterson told me that food was important in his home, growing up in Galashiels in the Scottish Borders. 'In our house, however, there was only my mum, dad, me and older brother David and so there was never a mad rush or pile ups to get to the table first. I used to love it when my mum baked at home. I was always very keen to help and lick the spoon! She made great fairy cakes, millionaire's shortbread – and her Christmas cake was baked by November. It was my job between then and Christmas to place slices of bread all round the cake, then re-wrap it. I have no idea why I did this but it was my job. When I removed the bread a week later it was rock hard!' Intrigued by this task (was this a Borders speciality?) I phoned Chris's mum Lyn to ask her about it and she told me it was a tip she had heard on *The Jimmy Young Show* – to put moisture back into the cake if you had overcooked it a little and you felt it might be a little dry. After the bread had been wrapped round the cake for a few days, it was like toast, so the moisture from the bread had gone into the cake. Top tip!

'As for favourite dishes from my childhood – I just wanted to eat whatever was in front of me as quickly as possible so I could then get out and play.' But Chris did tell me that though the food was traditional – stews, mince, soups – it was always good. 'But because I was a really fussy eater as a child, I would never try anything new, so plain fare suited me.' Sunday tea was always roast beef and Yorkshire puddings and New Year was always a steak pie.

'I can remember my granny making porridge with lots of sugar on it: it was great. My grandpa ate his only with salt.' The Patersons had fruit trees in their garden – apple, plum and damson – and Chris's mum would make jam from these, the damson one being a particular favourite.

Chris's granny and grandpa used to take him out for bar suppers quite often. 'We would go out on Saturdays and try new places as often as possible. There was a restaurant in Eddleston, just outside Peebles, which they often took me to when I was probably about seven or eight years old, and I can remember going there and getting my two favourite things: a bowl of cucumber and chips, with salad cream on the side. It was great. I couldn't get it anywhere else!'

Chris, perhaps unusually, hated pizza; 'I must have been the only kid that did. I was never a fan of beef olives either.' But he did always like soups, one of his mum's specials – a chicken and rice broth. His wife Claire also makes fabulous soups now, such as sweet potato and red pepper. His mum tried to teach him how to cook but 'as usual I didn't take too much of it in. Since then TV cooking shows and my wife have been more influential.'

As for producing Scottish dishes to cook now, he often cooks haggis and has porridge most mornings in the winter.

'I think a recipe that would sum up my childhood would be something sweet. I was really bad for only wanting sweet things.' His granny was from Selkirk, although she lived in Galashiels, near Chris's family. 'There was intense rivalry between Gala and Selkirk – most of it tongue in cheek. Into this friendly rivalry came the question of the Selkirk Bannie, which I used to love [it was called 'Selkirk Bannie' in the Borders], since it was loaded with fruit. I would eat that smeared thickly with butter in Galashiels, but with my Selkirk granny!'

Selkirk Bannock

makes 1 large bannock

Sue says: Here is my classic recipe for Chris.

900g/2 lb strong white flour
pinch of salt
2 x 7g sachets of easy-blend dried yeast
55g/2 oz caster sugar
approx. 500ml/18 fl oz semi-skimmed
    milk (or ½ water, ½ milk), warm

150g/5½ oz butter, softened
400g/14 oz sultanas
1 medium free-range egg, beaten,
    to glaze

Sift the flour and a pinch of salt into a bowl, then stir in the yeast and sugar. Add enough warm liquid to combine to a soft but not sticky dough. Turn onto a floured board and knead well for 10 minutes or so until smooth. Place in a bowl, cover and leave somewhere warm for 1–1½ hours, or until well risen.

Cut the softened butter into 4 then fold each piece into the dough, one at a time. Knead until thoroughly amalgamated. Then work in the sultanas, a handful at a time. Shape into a bannock: a round flattened dome about 28cm/11 in in diameter. Place on a buttered baking sheet and leave for about an hour, or until well risen.

Brush with the beaten egg to glaze, then bake in an oven preheated to 220°C/425°F/Gas 7 for 15 minutes. Reduce to 190°C/375°F/Gas 5 and continue to bake for 25–30 minutes, covering loosely with foil for the last 15–20 minutes to prevent the top burning. It is ready once it is golden brown all over and the base sounds hollow when tapped underneath. Leave to cool on a wire rack then slice and spread with butter.

index